Watercolour
Solutions

Watercolour
Solutions Albany Wiseman

COLLINS & BROWN

First published in Great Britain in 2003 by
Collins & Brown Limited
64 Brewery Road
London, N7 9NT
A member of Chrysalis Books plc

Distributed in the United States and Canada by Sterling
Publishing Co, 387 Park Avenue South, New York,
NY 10016, USA

9 8 7 6 5 4 3 2 1

British Library Cataloguing-in-Publication Data:
A catalogue record for this book is available from the
British Library.

ISBN 1 84340 037 5 (HB)

Conceived, edited and designed by Collins & Brown Limited
Editorial Director: Roger Bristow
Project Editor: Katie Hardwicke
Design Manager: Liz Wiffen
Design: Grade Design Consultants, London
Photographer: Ben Wray

Reproduction by Classicscan Pte Ltd, Singapore
Printed and bound by Times Offset, Malaysia

Contents

Introduction	6
Chapter 1: Materials and Equipment	**10**
Q1 What equipment do I need to get started?	12
Q2 What paper is suitable for watercolour?	13
Q3 What are the different weights of paper?	14
Q4 How do I stretch paper?	15
Q5 Can I paint on coloured paper?	16
Q6 What is the minimum number of brushes I need?	17
Q7 What are the different brushes used for?	18
Q8 What is the difference between pans and tubes?	20
Q9 What are concentrated watercolours?	20
Q10 What is body colour?	21
Q11 How do I use watercolour pencils?	22
Q12 What other equipment do I need?	24
Q13 What equipment do I need to paint out of doors?	24
Q14 How do I care for my equipment?	25
Chapter 2: Basic Techniques	**26**
Q15 How do I mix colours?	28
Q16 What is a limited palette?	30
Q17 How do I select my palette of colours?	32
Q18 What are warm and cool colours?	33
Q19 How do I mix greens?	34
Q20 How do I mix neutrals without white?	36
Q21 When should I use black?	37
Q22 What are shades, tints and tones?	38
Q23 What is monochrome?	39
Q24 How do I lay a flat wash?	40
Q25 How do I lay a gradated wash?	41
Q26 How do I lay a variegated wash?	42
Q27 How do I 'tone' paper?	43
Q28 How many washes can be laid over each other?	44
Q29 How do I stop the paint running?	45
Q30 How do I speed up drying time?	45
Chapter 3: Painting Techniques	**46**
Q31 What is underdrawing?	48

Q32 What is underpainting?   49
Q33 What is wet-on-wet?   50
Q34 What is blending?   51
Q35 What is wet-on-dry?   52
Q36 What is glazing?   53
Q37 What is dry-brush technique?   54
Q38 What is alla prima?   55
Q39 What is lifting out?   56
Q40 What is washing off?   57
Q41 What is back run?   57
Q42 What is distressing?   58
Q43 What is sgraffito?   58
Q44 What is broken colour?   59
Q45 What effects can be achieved with a sponge?   60
Q46 What is stippling?   60
Q47 What is spattering?   61
Q48 How do I add texture to a wash?   62
Q49 What other media can be used in watercolour?   64
Q50 What is overdrawing?   65
Q51 What is brush-ruling?   66
Q52 How do I leave white areas in a wash?   67
Q53 What are resist techniques?   68
Q54 How do I make colours appear more luminous?   70
Q55 How do I achieve an opaque effect?   70
Q56 How do I correct an area of a painting?   71

Chapter 4: Watercolour Subjects   72

Q57 How do I compose a painting?   74
Q58 What size should my painting be?   76
Q59 What is squaring or gridding up?   77
Q60 What are negative shapes?   77
Q61 What is perspective?   78
Q62 What is aerial perspective?   79
Q63 How do I light a subject?   80
Q64 How do I paint light and shade?   81
Q65 How do I convey the time of day?   82
Q66 How do I capture the qualities of evening light?   83
Q67 How do I simulate bright sunlight?   84

Q68 How do I paint shadows?   85
Q69 How do I paint landscapes?   86
Q70 How do I paint mountains?   87
Q71 How do I paint trees and foliage?   88
Q72 How do I paint autumnal scenes?   90
Q73 How do I convey the effects of rain and mist?   90
Q74 How do I convey the effects of snow and ice?   91
Q75 How do I paint skies?   92
Q76 How do I paint clouds?   94
Q77 How do I paint sunsets?   95
Q78 How do I paint stormy skies?   95
Q79 How do I paint seascapes?   96
Q80 How do I paint moving water   98
Q81 How do I paint rough water?   99
Q82 How do I make water appear transparent?   100
Q83 How do I paint reflections in water?   101
Q84 How do I paint buildings?   102
Q85 How do I paint interiors?   104
Q86 How do I paint flowers?   105
Q87 How do I paint still lifes?   106
Q88 How do I paint metal objects?   108
Q89 How do I paint glass objects?   108
Q90 How do I paint clothes and drapery?   109
Q91 How do I choose a pose?   110
Q92 How do I paint figure studies?   111
Q93 How do I paint children?   112
Q94 How do I paint portraits?   114
Q95 How do I paint a self-portrait?   116
Q96 How do I paint pale flesh tones?   117
Q97 How do I paint dark flesh tones?   117
Q98 How do I paint domestic animals?   118
Q99 How do I paint horses?   119
Q100 How do I paint birds?   120
Q101 How do I paint fish?   122

Glossary   124
Index   125
Acknowledgements   128

Introduction

As a painting medium, watercolour has very early beginnings. The ancient Egyptians and early Indian, Chinese and Persian civilizations used watercolour in their traditional art and decoration. Later, the German painter Albrecht Durër (1471–1528), became the first real master of the technique. In the seventeenth and eighteenth centuries, 'Grand Tour' artists carried their watercolours with them to record and paint their travels. Watercolour flourished as a medium and British artists, such as JMW Turner (1775–1851), John Sell Cotman (1782–1842) and Thomas Girtin (1775–1802) brought an awareness of the subtleties and nuances of watercolour to their patrons. A study of any of these artists is well worthwhile if you have come under the spell of watercolour painting – their techniques, colours and subject matter will provide a never-ending source of inspiration.

In this book, I have tried to answer some of the questions and make suggestions on how to approach the challenge of painting with watercolour. Although it may appear to be an uncomplicated technique, watercolour can be a frustrating medium with a 'mind of its own'! It is difficult to correct mistakes or make revisions and you will soon learn to resign yourself to starting again if things haven't gone quite as planned. However, the unpredictability of wet washes is part of watercolour's charm – applying a simple wash can give great pleasure. It is a medium that requires patience – waiting for washes to dry and analyzing and planning the effects of overlaid colour. With a little advice and practise, you will soon master the medium and regain control to produce pictures full of light, spontaneity and colour.

To achieve success, you need to consider several factors before you even start to paint. Think about your choice of paper – the weight, texture and tone will all have a bearing on how the wash is absorbed, whether edges will be blurred or crisp, and how colours will blend and dry. Look at your subject carefully and plan which techniques will be suitable – most resist techniques need to be applied at the start of the painting in order to retain the pure white of the paper. Think about your palette of colours and whether it suits the mood of the subject – is it warm or cool, are there neutrals and shadows, or a range of natural greens? When mixing your washes, always bear in mind that watercolour dries lighter than when it is applied, and always work from light to dark, building up colours and tones with subtlety. You can, of course, combine watercolour with gouache, or body colour, to add opaque, lighter colour over darks – a technique especially suited to figure paintings.

Throughout the book short projects are included in order to illustrate particular techniques or subject matter. You can either follow these step-by-step instructions in order to practise techniques and build confidence, or use them as reference for your own paintings. Everyone's palette of colours vary, the paints that I use in the step-by-step exercises are Schminke and Winsor and Newton Artist's Quality pans and you will find similar colours (some under different names) in most paint manufacturer's ranges.

I hope that the one hundred and one questions will help both beginners and more experienced painters to face the watercolour challenge. Due to the pressures of space, some subjects may warrant more comprehensive study and I hope that you will be encouraged to investigate further where necessary. The most important points to bear in mind are to keep it simple and paint as much as possible to build your confidence.

After many years, I am still learning and experimenting – it is the nature of the creative process.

Enjoy your journey.

Albany Wiseman

Chapter 1: Materials and Equipment

The vast array of enticing paints, papers and brushes that confronts you in any art supply store can appear confusing, especially if you are choosing your equipment for the first time. My advice is to keep things simple with a small selection of brushes, a basic palette of colours and some paper. This chapter gives you the background information to make the right choices and provides you with a few additional ideas in order to extend your range of techniques.

Q1 What equipment do I need to get started?

A | A small selection of materials is all you need to start painting. You will need paper or a sketchbook (see opposite), an HB or 2B pencil for making preliminary sketches or underdrawings, a soft putty eraser and a selection of pans or tubes of watercolour paint, and a few brushes. You will also need a palette and a water pot with a separate supply of clean water, if painting on location. A drawing board and sloping easel will provide you with a firm surface that can be tilted to lie flat or at an angle. Lightweight tripod easels are available for painting outdoors, which leave your hands free to mix colours and assess your work.

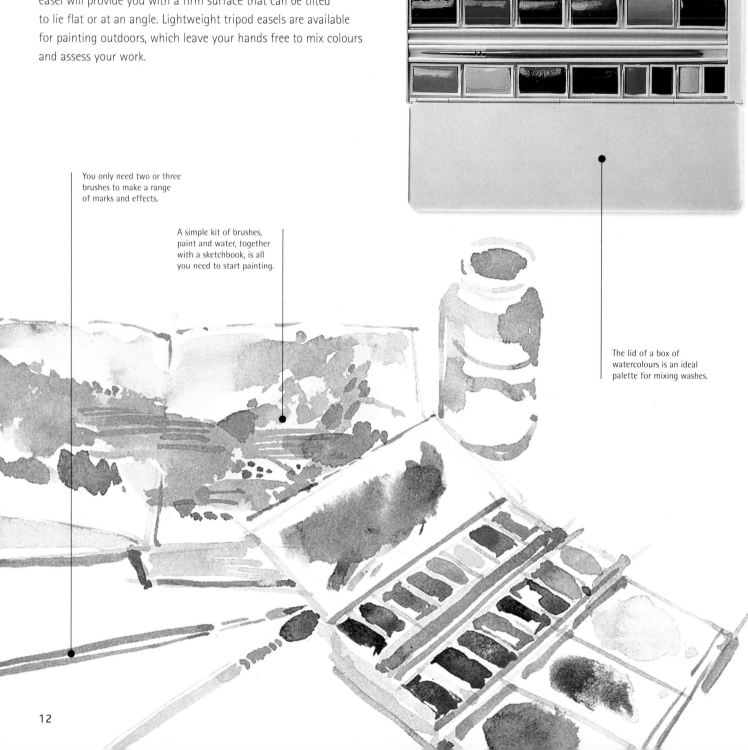

You only need two or three brushes to make a range of marks and effects.

A simple kit of brushes, paint and water, together with a sketchbook, is all you need to start painting.

The lid of a box of watercolours is an ideal palette for mixing washes.

Q2 What paper is suitable for watercolour?

A | **There are three main types of paper with different surfaces – rough, NOT or cold-pressed (CP), and hot-pressed (HP).** Paper is also graded by weight. Different surfaces and weights of papers affect how the paint adheres and hence suit different painting styles. A heavy paper (over 300lb) will not require stretching (see Question 4). Stretching paper is advised for lighter weight papers and hot-pressed papers to avoid cockling as washes of paint dry.

Rough paper has a natural, grainy surface that gives texture and adds sparkle to paintings. Cold-pressed paper is lightly textured and is a good general paper. Hot-pressed paper has a smooth surface which enables you to paint in more detail.

Paper is available in rolls, sheets and pads or blocks of different sizes. There are many different brands of paper. It is worth experimenting with a few to find one that suits your painting style. Tinted watercolour paper is also available. For longevity, choose archival quality paper, preferably made from 100% cotton rag. Acid-free paper will not yellow over time. Watercolour paper cannot be reused, as the various ingredients of watercolour paint mean that the paint adheres permanently to the paper surface.

Hot-pressed
A smooth surface that absorbs the paint slowly. It is suited to wet washes and gives a flat finish. Ideal for fine details.

Cold-pressed
A slightly textured surface that gives uneven edges. It is suited to most watercolour techniques.

Rough
A pitted surface that gives a textured finish. It is suited to most techniques and is ideal for sgraffito.

Large sheets of watercolour paper are available loose or in blocks and are suited to studio or easel work.

A small, spiral bound sketchbook will fit easily into a pocket or bag and will lay flat when in use.

Q3 What are the different weights of paper?

A It may appear confusing to be confronted with the many varieties of paper, together with the wide choice of weights. Papers are made and measured by the weight of a ream. This figure is expressed in pounds or grams per square meter (gsm). The standard paper weights are: 90lb (185gsm),

140lb (300gsm) and 300lb (640gsm). The heavier the weight, the thicker the paper. Lighter paper, for example 90lb, will need to be stretched to prevent cockling (see opposite). The chart below describes the different types and weights of paper, their characteristics and suitability:

Type	Weight	Characteristics
Hot-pressed	90–300lb	Good for very wet washes, produces a flat, smooth finish, with slow absorption. Stretch all paper under 140lb before use.
Cold-pressed	90lb, 140lb	Good for most watercolour techniques except sgraffito, gives an even finish with slight texture. You will need to stretch the paper before use.
Cold-pressed	300lb	Suitable for sgraffito and other techniques that require heavy handling, it is slightly textured, with slow absorption. No need to stretch paper.
Rough	90lb, 140lb	Good for most techniques other than those requiring fine detail due to the pitted surface. It is quite absorbent. You will need to stretch the paper before use.
Rough	300lb and above	Good for vigorous techniques, such as sgraffito. It has a rough finish with slow absorption. You do not need to stretch the paper.

Left: A wash applied to a heavy, rough paper will be absorbed slowly to dry with soft edges.

Below: A wash applied to thin, smooth paper will cause the paper to cockle and the paint to dry in irregular pools and patches.

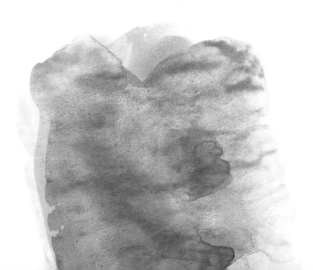

Q4 How do I stretch paper?

A To prevent them from cockling when a wash is applied, most lightweight papers (those under 140lb) will need to be stretched before you start to paint. You will need a heavy board that will not bend or warp when water is applied. Cut your paper to the required size before you start and ensure that the board is larger than the paper. Use gummed tape rather than cellulose masking tape. Stretching paper is not a difficult task and it only requires a little pre-planning and patience. You should allow approximately 8–10 hours for the paper to dry out thoroughly before you apply your first wash of paint.

Project

MATERIALS Heavy wooden board, sheet of watercolour paper, scissors, gummed paper tape, sponge, tray of water

1 Cut the paper to the required size and lay it flat on the board. Leave enough margin around all sides for the paper tape.

2 Cut four strips of gummed tape for each side of the piece of paper. Make the strips slightly longer than the paper.

3 Lay the paper flat in a tray or sink of clean water and immerse for a few minutes. Make sure that it is evenly wet but not soaking. Lift it out and drain any excess water.

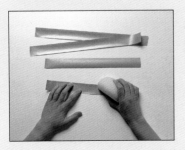

4 With a damp, clean sponge moisten the adhesive side of the paper tape on a flat surface.

5 Lay the wet paper flat on the board, smoothing out any crinkles. Tape the paper to the board, starting with the long sides, ensuring that the paper is pulled taut.

6 Lay the board flat and allow to dry completely, preferably overnight. Any creases will flatten out as the paper dries.

Q5 Can I paint on coloured paper?

A | **Watercolour achieves its transparent quality partly from the medium itself and partly from the white paper which adds to its luminosity.** However, it is possible to use alternative papers that are coloured or toned. You may need to use opaque white gouache to achieve light or white areas of the painting.

There are many different papers available and many different colours, ranging from grey and green to blues and browns, but you will need to use light tints if selecting a coloured paper. Your choice may be governed by the subject matter and the feel of the painting, for example a cool blue for a sky study, or pale grey of a cold, rainy landscape. Warm creams and browns are suitable for figure studies.

I chose a tinted handmade paper known as Turner's blue, for this painting. The tone unifies the shaded buildings.

Ordinary brown wrapping or kraft paper stretches well to produce a flat, receptive working surface. I drew this figure in sanguine pencil, adding loose watercolour and gouache washes on top.

Q6 What is the minimum number of brushes I need?

A There are many brushes available, ranging in size from 000 to 24, with a choice of natural, synthetic or mixed fibres. When purchasing your brushes you need to consider the material they are made from, their size and shape. Natural fibres of hair or bristle are the more expensive choice but they will retain their shape and last well if looked after. Synthetic fibres are considerably cheaper but will need to be replaced more regularly. A good compromise is a mixed fibre brush, which benefits from the advantages of a natural brush but at a fraction of the cost.

You do not need to purchase a whole set of brushes. The smallest brushes sized 000, for example, are suitable for very fine detailing and are of limited use. Purchase the best that you can within your budget and look after them well (see Question 14). Professional artists will often have just three favourite round brushes, such as Nos. 3, 5 and 8, a couple of squirrel brushes which hold plenty of water and are good for broad washes, and a mop brush which is also good for laying washes. You can add more unusual brushes to suit your subject matter or style of painting (see Question 7).

A mop brush is ideal for laying broad areas of colour or washes and for moving or blending wet paint on the paper.

A squirrel brush holds a generous amount of wash and forms a good point for defining broad shapes.

A No. 5 round brush is a good all-round brush, ideal for bands of colour and for painting finer details using the point.

Q7 What are the different brushes used for?

A Round brushes are the most common and frequently-used watercolour brushes, but there is a great variety of shapes that you can call upon for special techniques or unusual effects. A flat brush is invaluable for laying broad washes of an even tone. For feathered effects use a fan brush or a rigger, which allows you to paint in fine detail and is suitable for twigs and leaves. Chinese brushes are available in different sizes and are well-suited to laying washes. They form perfect points, too, and are good for detail.

I used a flat brush to lay a soft wash for the background hills, using the end of the brush to add streaks to break up the even tone.

I added loose strokes of colour to the foreground, again using the side and end of the flat brush to vary the size of the marks and add textural interest.

I was drawn to the strong horizontal lines of this old slate quarry. I used a minimum of three brushes – a flat, a mop and a small round – to capture the scene.

I used a flat brush to follow the bold lines of the iron rafters and a small round brush for the regular pattern of the stone building.

Chinese brushes hold a lot of water and maintain a fine point. They are good for calligraphic work and also for laying washes.

Flat brushes are useful for laying washes or broad areas of colour.

Rigger brushes are long-haired and good for fine detail.

Fan brushes produce delicate, feathery lines, ideal for foliage or wispy clouds.

Q8 What is the difference between pans and tubes?

A | Watercolour paint is available in pans or tubes – the highest grade is artist's colour. Pans or half-pans contain a block of semi-moist paint. They are the most practical, especially for working outdoors, as they are easy to transport and you can see the colours at a glance. Tube paint contains more dextrin, gum arabic and glycerine, which makes them less likely to dry-up than pan colour. Tube paint is useful for mixing large washes.

Try to buy artist's quality paints, even if this means that you have less variety in your palette. It is a false economy to use cheaper and inferior materials.

Watercolour is available as tubes, pans and half-pans of paint. You can also buy a china 'block' of paint which is ideal for mixing large washes.

TIP - If pan colours dry, a small drop of honey or glycerine will help to moisten the colour.

Q9 What are concentrated watercolours?

A | Concentrated, or liquid, watercolours are available in small bottles with a rubber dropper or dispenser. They are intense and vibrant colours made from chemical dyes, often used by illustrators and textile designers for airbrush work or in technical pens. Some interesting effects can be made by dropping pure colour onto a wet wash, but they are not a substitute for artist's watercolours.

The intensity of the colours makes them undesirable for most landscape painting, but ideal for flower studies or still lifes.

The strong, vibrant nature of concentrated watercolours lend themselves to flower studies.

Concentrated watercolour will bleed and feather when dropped on to wet paper.

Q10 What is body colour?

A **Body colour, or 'gouache', is a water-based opaque paint.** Pure watercolour has a transparency, which is one of its main qualities, that negates the use of white and many purists will not use white in watercolour.

Gouache is available in tubes of colours or as Chinese white, which can be mixed with traditional watercolours to create opaque colour. Use a separate palette for mixing and tube watercolour paints as pans can lose their transparency. Gouache will be shown to advantage on a tinted or toned paper.

The great English watercolour painter, JMW Turner, introduced opaque white to a picture, using it in 'local' areas. It can be used for clouds, white sails, to describe the pattern of fur or feathers, or simply as a highlight in a sunlit scene.

For this portrait study, I used white gouache to add highlights to the dress and blended this to give opacity to the skin tones.

I used gouache to add lights over darks in this sunlit landscape, mixing the greens in a separate palette with Chinese white. I painted on to a warm toned paper, using sanguine pencil for my initial sketch.

Q11 How do I use watercolour pencils?

A | Water-soluble pencils are a very useful addition to your outdoor sketching equipment. You can use them to draw or sketch the main elements of your composition, using hatching or shading to give tone and depth. These areas can then be blended on the paper with a damp brush or wetted finger with more control than traditional watercolour paint or washes. Alternatively, you can combine them with watercolour washes. Apply the pencil over a damp wash for a soft, feathered line or onto a dry wash for more precise detailing.

Blending can be achieved without wetting, but large areas or washes of colour are obviously difficult to produce. Watercolour pencils can be used on any paper surface, but for best results choose a cold- or hot-pressed paper. Select your own colours by buying them separately.

You can make detailed sketches or even finished paintings using watercolour pencils with a brush and supply of water. I combined dry pencil marks with wetted, blended marks to give the impression of the aged and weathered stonework on this church.

I smudged and blended the overlaid marks on the building using a wetted finger.

Scribbled, unblended marks of overlaid colour give a loose impression of the trees and bushes.

Q12 What other equipment do I need?

A| Paper, paint, a brush and clean water are all the basics that you need to start painting, but in order to expand your repertoire of techniques and enjoy watercolour to the full, there are a few additional pieces of equipment that will soon become part of your painting kit. A sponge (natural or synthetic) is invaluable for damping paper, lifting-off and laying washes, blotting paper or kitchen paper is essential for mopping up runs or lifting-off washes, cotton buds are useful for lifting-off in smaller, more detailed areas. For textural techniques you will need a toothbrush for spattering paint. Masking fluid is essential for protecting the underlying paper from washes (see Question 53) and masking tape acts in a similar way to create defined edges.

Keep tissues, cotton swabs, old brushes, toothbrushes and sponges close to hand when in the studio or on location.

Q13 What equipment do I need to paint outdoors?

A| The main requirement is that the equipment is light and easily carried. The essentials should include a sketching stool or lightweight easel, paper or a sketchbook, HB, 2B or 3B pencils, an eraser, tubes or pans of watercolour paint, a good palette, a selection of 3 or 4 brushes (retractable brushes are available), a water container with spare water bottle, tissues, a sponge and a satchel. These are the basics, in addition you should always carry a small sketchbook for notes and preliminary thumbnail sketches, together with a selection of watercolour pencils.

Other equipment may include a drawing board – some lightweight versions made from foam board are available, as are boards with carrying straps. Portable painting trolleys on wheels with an easel combined with a seat are available.

Select your paper or sketchbook carefully. Some papers will need to be stretched beforehand but you can purchase pads or blocks of paper that do not require stretching. A heavier weight of paper will prevent cockling. On less expensive papers it is preferable not to wash right up to the edge of the paper.

The two main problems with outdoor painting are wind and rain. Take some clips to hold down your work and a cover, such as a sheet of plastic or bubble wrap, to protect the work from rain drops. If you are in the hot sun, protect your head with a sun hat and use a high factor sun cream.

A sketchbook is easily transportable and gives you the opportunity to make notes or finished paintings in one place.

A lightweight stool and easel will make painting on location more comfortable and enjoyable. Invest in a bag or satchel for your sketchbook, paints and brushes and don't forget a hat!

Q14 How do I care for my equipment?

A | The most important items to keep clean are your brushes. They are often expensive but with care they can last for many years. The following list of 'dos and don'ts' will help you to keep your equipment in perfect order:

Do

- Clean your brushes thoroughly after use by holding the brush under warm running water and rinsing until the water runs clear.
- Put brushes away after use (in Spain on one occasion my beautiful No. 12 sable was eaten by mice!), make sure that they are thoroughly dry before storing for any length of time.
- Store your brushes standing in a jar or container with the points up or suspend them from a shelf with sticky putty (blu tack).
- Clean your palette after every painting session.
- Replace lids on tubes and close lids of watercolour paint boxes.

Don't

- Leave brushes standing in the water pot, they will lose their 'spring' and point.
- Store brushes with the points down.
- Leave watercolour pigment to dry. Add a few drops of glycerine or honey to restore the moisture or spray with water.

Chapter 2: Basic Techniques

Watercolour paintings gain their particular characteristics from the subtle layering of washes and blends of colours. This chapter explores the principles behind mixing colours and laying simple washes, helping you to understand how to achieve a wide range of natural colours from a limited palette and lay the foundations for a successful painting.

Q15 How do I mix colours?

A | A basic knowledge of colour theory is necessary in order to create a palette of colours.

The colour wheel shows a simple way of understanding mixing and the relationship of one colour to another.

Primary colours are red, yellow and blue. These colours cannot be made from other colours, but all other colours, in theory, can be mixed from them.

Secondary colours are the mixes made by combining different combinations of the three primary colours: red and yellow make orange; red and blue make violet; blue and yellow make green.

Tertiary colours are a mix of one primary and an adjacent secondary, making a third, intermediate mix which might be a yellow-green or blue-violet.

To help you to understand how colours can be created, it is worth painting your own colour wheel, starting with the primary colours from ready-made pigments and then mixing the secondary and tertiary colours. You will soon discover that there are many different mixes that can be created with different dilutions of water to paint and different proportions of pigment and wash.

When mixing colours and creating washes, try to restrict your mixes to just three colours – too many colours can result in a muddy mix. An enormous variety of greens can be made from blues, yellows and browns (see Question 19).

Always keep your water clean and mix a generous amount of pigment with lots of water. Never mix a colour on the paper, always on a palette.

This simple colour wheel shows the primary and secondary colours and their relationships. Complementary colours are those that are opposite each other on the wheel – red and green, violet and yellow, blue and orange. When used together, these colours appear stronger and can be used to good effect in composition.

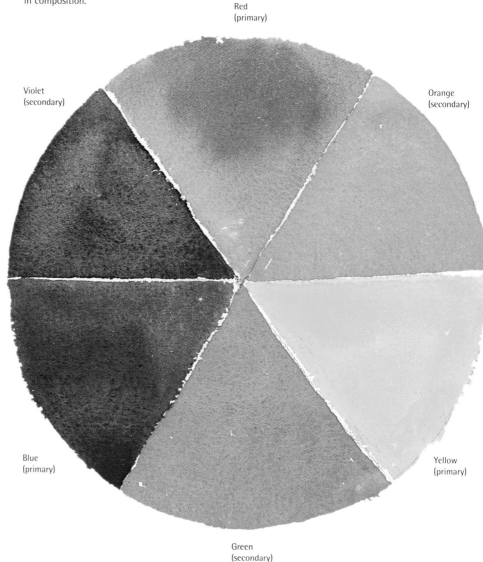

Red
(primary)

Violet
(secondary)

Orange
(secondary)

Blue
(primary)

Yellow
(primary)

Green
(secondary)

These examples show how you can mix secondary colours from three primary watercolour paints.

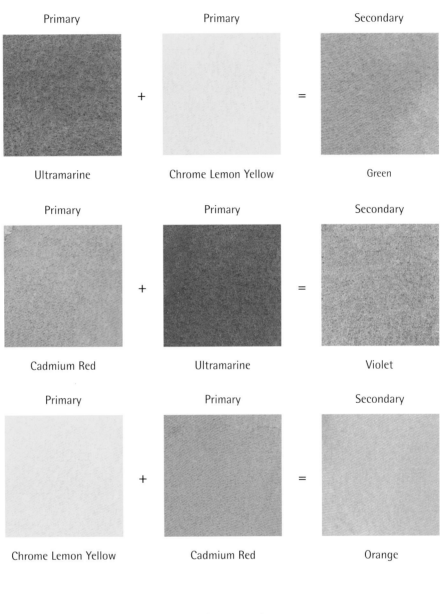

Primary		Primary		Secondary
Ultramarine	+	Chrome Lemon Yellow	=	Green
Cadmium Red	+	Ultramarine	=	Violet
Chrome Lemon Yellow	+	Cadmium Red	=	Orange

This example shows how you can use a mixed secondary – orange – together with a manufactured green, to produce a neutral shade, sometimes called a tertiary colour.

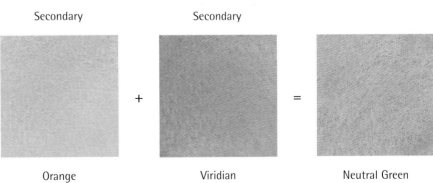

Secondary		Secondary		
Orange	+	Viridian	=	Neutral Green

Q16 What is a limited palette?

A | It is possible to paint fine watercolours using mixes created from just the three primary colours: **red, yellow and blue.** These can be mixed to make secondary and tertiary hues to give you a surprisingly varied palette (see Question 15). A small, limited palette of five colours (blue, yellow, red, brown and green) encourages experimentation and mixing, and will help you to understand how colours work and how to achieve your own, customized mix. Practise mixing colours in different dilutions and proportions – you will be amazed at the range of tones and hues that you can achieve with just a small selection of colours.

A basic palette could include:

Blues: French ultramarine, cobalt (extras: cerulean and ultramarine violet)
Yellows: cadmium lemon, yellow ochre or raw sienna (extras: Naples yellow, (opaque) gamboge or aureolin)
Reds: cadmium red, light red, alizarin crimson (extras: Venetian red)
Brown: burnt umber, sepia
Green: viridian, sap green

This loose, landscape study was painted alla prima, using just three colours – cobalt blue, ultramarine and cadmium lemon – to mix the different tones of bright yellow-greens that are used for the building and foliage. A darker mix, using more blue, was used for the stronger green of the trees. A limited palette is ideally suited to working at speed, recording your impressions with just a few mixes and simple brushstrokes.

Project

MATERIALS Rough paper 140lb (300gsm), 4B pencil, medium squirrel brush, No. 4 sable, watercolour paints

This landscape was painted using the primary colours: gamboge (yellow), light red and cobalt blue. Always test your mixes first on a piece of scrap paper and remember that watercolour paint is lighter when dry.

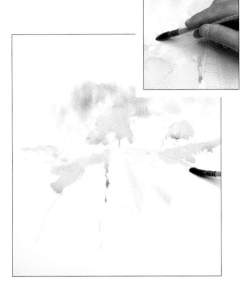

1 Lightly sketch in the composition. Wet the paper and mix a light blue wash of cobalt blue. Use a medium squirrel brush to apply the wash to the sky, leaving some areas white to represent clouds. Use the wash to add tone to the road in the foreground. Mix a neutral tone from cobalt and light red and apply to the sky to add depth.

2 Mix a very light green from gamboge and cobalt blue, in approximate proportions of 3:1. Apply this to the trees and hillside. **Inset:** Make a thin, watery wash of light red and apply this over the blue on the road and roofs to add a warm tone.

3 Wet the tree areas, then mix a green wash from cobalt blue and gamboge and apply with a No. 4 sable brush. Introduce some detail to the roof using a pure wash of light red. Mix gamboge and light red to make a pale orange wash for the warm terracotta of the buildings.

4 Mix a dark purple from cobalt with a touch of light red and add the window details and areas of shadow on the buildings.

5 The finished painting shows how a subtle depth of colour can be achieved with varied mixes of just three colours.

Variation
This scene was painted with a warm palette of cobalt blue, alizarin crimson and raw sienna.

Q17 How do I select my palette of colours?

A | Most paint manufacturers have over 100 colours to choose from, and this choice can be bewildering for a newcomer. You can, of course, create a painting using ready-mixed paint colours but the result would appear unnatural and much of the joy of watercolour is derived from personalizing your own paintings with individual mixes. When selecting colours include a warm and cool tone of the hue. Your choice of colours may also be determined by your subject matter: landscapes, still lifes and figure studies all require a different balance of colours. Start with a basic palette (see Question 16) and add extra paints depending on the mood, colour temperature (see opposite) and subject matter.

The warm reds and oranges of these flowers were mixed from cadmium red, cadmium lemon, raw sienna and light red. Flower paintings often call for almost pure pigment to match the natural intensity of the colours.

Landscapes are generally dominated by greens, but rather than buy ready-mixed colours, you will achieve a much more natural hue by mixing your own from different combinations of blue and yellow (see Question 19).

Figure studies require a palette often based on warm flesh tones, such as light red, raw sienna and alizarin crimson. I also use a cool green – terre verte – for the shadow areas.

Q18 What are warm and cool colours?

A | **A hue can be described as having a colour 'temperature'.** Reds, oranges and yellows are clearly warm colours, and blues, greens and purples are cool colours. In painting, colour pigments vary and it is possible to purchase and mix colours that have a different temperature bias. For example, Winsor blue has a cool bias, whereas French ultramarine has a warm bias; cadmium red is a warm red, but alizarin crimson has a bluer bias and is described as cool.

These qualities can be useful if you wish to portray a particular feel or atmosphere in your painting. Warm and cool colours (reds and blues, for example) can be used as important compositional elements in a painting. Colour temperature is an important factor to consider when planning a painting. It affects the composition and atmosphere of a picture. Warm colours appear to advance, whilst cool colours recede. A warm palette will create a lively image, whereas a cool palette will be more subdued. Warm colours can be used to draw the eye into a painting or create a focal point (see Question 57).

By mixing colours with a similar temperature bias you can create muted mixes that maintain harmony across the painting.

The colour mixes below show how different greens can be mixed from warm and cool blues and yellows.

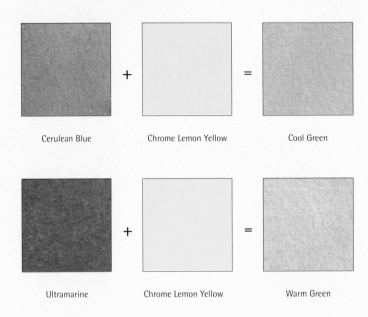

Cerulean Blue + Chrome Lemon Yellow = Cool Green

Ultramarine + Chrome Lemon Yellow = Warm Green

This landscape is predominantly cool in tone, using mixes of sap green and cerulean blue with Payne's grey for the shadow areas.

The warmth of the buildings was created using washes of ochre, raw sienna and light red with alizarin crimson. I used a cool blue-green for the sky to increase the contrast between foreground and background.

33

Q19 How do I mix greens?

A| The variety of shades and tints of green that can be seen in nature are countless. It is a colour that needs to be used with caution, as it is all too easy to dip into a ready-made green on your palette with a very unnatural result. There are approximately 15 to 20 different ready-mixed pans and tubes of greens in the watercolour range – too many to include in the everyday palette. Selecting and mixing your own is the solution.

A mix of any blue and yellow will make a variety of tints and hues of green, depending on the proportions of water to pigment and the ratio of pigments. Ultramarine is a good blue to use for natural mixes. Good yellows to include for mixing are: gamboge, chrome lemon, aureolin. Ultramarine and aureolin gives a bright spring green.

Ready-made greens that are natural transparent colours are viridian and sap green, more opaque colours are Hooker's green and chromium oxide green. Use these in mixes, rather than on their own. May green is a very bright, lime green that is ideal for the fresh new buds of spring.

Viridian mixed with a warm colour, such as burnt sienna, alizarin crimson or light red, becomes a soft, dark tone.

Ultramarine and raw sienna give an olive green. Mixed with chrome lemon it produces a soft green.

 +  =

Viridian   Light Red

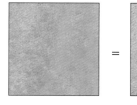 +  =

Ultramarine   Raw Sienna

 +  =

Viridian   Alizarin Crimson

 +  =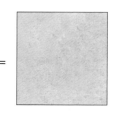

Ultramarine   Chrome Lemon Yellow

 + =

Viridian   Burnt Sienna

The light spring greens were mixed from cadmium lemon and a little cobalt blue.

I darkened the mix with a little Payne's grey for the shadows in the foreground.

This woodland scene of dappled light falling through the trees and their reflections in the river makes for a pleasing study in greens. I used sap green and mixed cadmium lemon with cobalt blue for a further range of colours.

Q20 How do I mix neutrals without white?

A You do not need to add white to a primary or secondary colour in order to produce a muted, neutral tone. Any combination of two of the three primary colours – red, blue and yellow – will make a variation of a neutral grey. For example, viridian mixed with light red produces a deep green-brown. Ultramarine violet and burnt umber create a good colour for shadow areas. Alizarin crimson and ultramarine make a neutral cloud colour. Raw sienna and cobalt blue will give you a wide range of primary, secondary and tertiary tones of blues, olives, greens and yellows that are ideal for landscapes.

Neutral colours are available ready-made and can be a useful addition to your palette. The colour samples and swatches illustrated right show some readily available neutral colours: neutral tint, Payne's grey, Davy's grey, indigo and ultramarine violet – a very useful colour for shadows.

The other swatches show neutral mixes from the primaries, some warm and some cool.

Neutral Tint   Payne's Grey   Davy's Grey

Indigo   Ultramarine Violet

These subtle, neutral colours are available ready-made. They can either be used on their own or in mixes and are especially useful for muted shadows.

The subdued mood of this study is enhanced by the use of neutral tones, both ready-made and mixed.

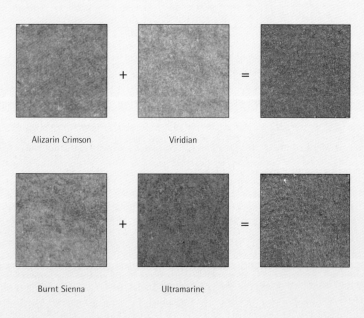

Alizarin Crimson   +   Viridian   =

Burnt Sienna   +   Ultramarine   =

The examples above show neutral colours created by mixing complementary colours – red and green, and orange and blue.

Q21 When should I use black?

A | Traditionally, black was not recommended as part of the watercolour painter's palette, as it can give a muddy or turbid colour when mixed with other paints. Pure black rarely occurs in landscape painting and you will find that neutral tones will render shadows much more effectively than adding black to your mixes. However, there are some instances where you may require a solid black. Lamp black is probably the 'cleanest' and clearest black and can be used as a thin underwash for certain subjects. It is a greyish black, consisting of pure carbon.

Ivory black, made from bone, is very dense and can lead to muddy colour if used with a strong element of other pigments.

There are black water-soluble pencils which can be used to advantage when out sketching and making tonal drawings.

For this monochrome study, I mixed an underwash of lamp black, applying the details with a black pencil.

In this study, I used ivory black for the dense colour of the shadowed pine needles.

A light wash of lamp black has been used to define the sky and the shadowed side of the building.

A soft, black pencil has been used to overdraw details and foreground texture.

Q22 What are shades, tints and tones?

A| Hue is another word used by artists to describe pure colour. A shade is a hue that has been darkened. A tint is a hue that has been lightened. Tone is the value of a colour, whether it is light or dark, and can be judged on a tonal scale. Tonal values are very important in painting, where light and shade are used to define objects and give them depth and form. The effect of tone can best be seen in monochrome paintings (see opposite), using shades and tints of just one colour.

The watercolour artist creates shades and tints where mixes are diluted or darkened as the painting develops. The balance of these colours and their progression from light to dark, will help to build a realistic impression of light and shade, depth and form.

To understand the range of shades and tints that can be created from one colour, try to make your own tonal scale. Start with a pure tube colour then darken this either with the addition of black or by adding a complimentary colour. At the other end of the scale, add white to lighten the colour to create tints or dilute the colour with water to create a paler wash, increasing the amount of water each time. Shades and tints can also be created by layering washes, or applying glazes, of the same colour.

Create your own tonal scale by darkening and lightening pure pigment.

← ——— Shades ——— →   Pure colour   ← ——— Tints ——— →

A darker shade of the wash has been used on the shadowed side of the wall.

The tints of colour in the foreground suggest a subtle change in tone.

This simple painting uses a range of tones to convey light and shade, and form.

Q23 What is monochrome?

A **Monochrome is the use of a single colour in a painting to depict the different effects of light and shade.**
Painting in monochrome is well-suited to studies where strong contrasts of light and shade are required, for example in sunlit scenes. Tonal still lifes are also good subjects, where the play of light and the density of the objects lend themselves to a simple and dramatic approach.

When working in monochrome, start with the lightest tones and work up to the darker areas. You can achieve a finished painting with just three or four simple washes of one colour, or by overlaying washes of one colour to build up the intensity of the hue.

The darkest tone is used for the recessed, shadow areas in the eyes and under the chin.

I left white paper to represent the highlights.

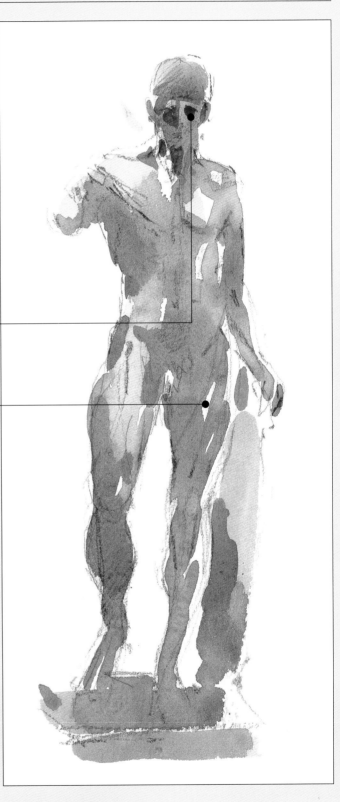

I used tones of Payne's grey for this quick study, looking down steps to an archway. The darkest tone is used to define the shadow beneath the arch, in contrast to the bright, sunlit wall.

I painted this cast using washes of burnt umber, starting with a light underwash and adding darker tones to suggest the form of the body.

Q24 How do I lay a flat wash?

Project

MATERIALS Arches rough paper 140lb (300gsm), sponge, flat brush, watercolour paint

A | **A flat wash is a broad area of colour applied with a large brush.** You will have to work quickly to keep the strokes even and it is helpful to dampen the paper first so that the paint moves more readily. Before you start, mix a large amount of wash and test the colour on spare paper, dampen the paper with clean water and a sponge, and load a large brush, such as a flat brush or mop brush. Tilt the board or paper slightly to help the paint to blend and apply the wash quickly with broad sweeps working back and forth across the paper, gathering any runs as you go. Continue to cover the paper in alternate directions.

A flat wash can be used as an underpainting or for toning the paper to provide a neutral midtone that unifies the image. This is especially useful for still lifes or figure studies, where the background helps to set the mood of the painting. A pale wash can also be used to reduce the glare of the paper if you are working in very bright sunlight.

For this harbour scene I first laid a soft, very pale flat wash of raw sienna to unify the image and provide a warm overall background tone.

To ensure that the wash is an even tone, you will need to work quickly, keeping the brushstrokes even. The thinner the wash the flatter it will dry.

1 Lightly dampen the paper with a clean, moist sponge to cover the wash area. Mix a thin wash of ultramarine and load the brush. Tilt the paper slightly and lay a stroke across the top of the paper. Bring the brush back across the paper and continue backwards and forwards.

2 Continue down the paper, working quickly and collecting any paint that has gathered at the base of a stroke. Lay the paper flat once the wash is complete and allow to dry.

Q25 How do I lay a gradated wash?

A | A gradated wash is a single colour wash that has subtle changes in intensity or tone, changing from dark to light down the paper. It is applied in a similar way to a flat wash (see opposite), diluting the wash further with each stroke. Start by damping the paper with clean water and a sponge, mix a generous amount of wash and start at the top with a stroke of colour, now gradually remove the colour from the brush by squeezing it and then dip it in water and continue with a few more strokes, working back and forth across the paper, diluting the wash as you go. The colour will gradate more if the paper or board is tilted. Gradated washes can be used for a cloudless sky.

Project

MATERIALS Arches rough paper 140lb (300gsm), sponge, mop brush, watercolour paint

Apply the wash in a similar way to a flat wash (see opposite), but lighten the wash as you move down the paper.

1 Lightly dampen the paper with a clean, moist sponge. Mix a wash of cerulean and load the mop brush. Lay a stroke of colour from left to right across the top of the paper, then back and forth as you progress down. Add more water to the brush, rather than paint, to thin the wash as you go.

2 Continue to move down the paper, working quickly to avoid streaking or dry edges. Once complete, lay the paper flat and allow to dry. The wash should appear to gradate from dark to light down the paper.

In this landscape study I used a gradated wash in the sky, fading the colour towards the horizon to give a sense of distance and suggest aerial perspective.

Q26 How do I lay a variegated wash?

A A two-colour or variegated wash involving more than one colour, is less predictable or controllable than flat or gradated washes. By applying two washes together and allowing the colours to move and blend freely, you will achieve some subtle and effective results. Start by damping the paper lightly with clean water. Then, mix two palettes of the colours that you wish to blend and apply a wash of the first colour. While still wet and with clean colour, apply the second wash adjacent to the first. Take care not to move the brush about, but tilt the paper slightly to encourage the colours to merge naturally.

A variegated wash has many uses, from the range of colours in a sunset to the subtle skin tones of a portrait study.

This study from my Moroccan sketchbook shows the subtle changes in the sky at dusk. I used a variegated wash to suggest the warm glow of the setting sun along the horizon, with a darker blue at the top.

Project

MATERIALS Arches rough paper 140lb (300gsm), sponge, No. 8 squirrel brush, watercolour paints

You can encourage two washes to blend together by turning the paper while the paint is still damp.

1 Lightly dampen the paper with a clean, moist sponge. Mix a thin red wash from alizarin crimson and load the brush. Lay a wash of red on the top half of the paper.

2 Turn the paper upside down and lay a wash of cadmium yellow, stopping at the edge of the red wash. The two washes will start to blend together. You can turn the paper again to encourage the mix if necessary.

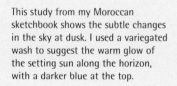

3 Leave the washes to dry. The finished wash will be lighter and the soft blend between the two colours will be subtle.

Q27 How do I 'tone' paper?

A| **White watercolour paper can be slightly toned by applying a pale wash of colour.** This can help to take away the glare when working in bright sunshine, or it can be used as a midtone to give a unifying effect to a painting. Light tones will help to achieve colour 'key' and balance.

Pre-tinted papers are available (see Question 5) but the advantage of toning your own paper is that you can mix your own strength of tint. An acrylic wash can be used to give a permanent tone. Apply flat washes (see Question 24) for an even tone. Stretch the paper first. Tea or coffee can also be used to permanently stain the paper.

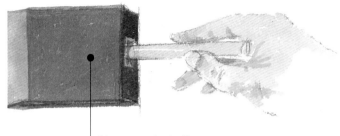

A large sponge brush will make the application of a broad wash much easier.

I applied a flat wash of raw sienna over the entire picture. By using raw sienna in the subsequent mixes, the picture has an inherent harmony that reflects the calm nature of the scene.

I suggested the hazy sun by lightly rubbing the wash with sandpaper.

Q28 How many washes can be laid over each other?

Project

MATERIALS   Arches rough paper 300gsm (140lb), sponge, No. 2 and No. 8 squirrel brushes, watercolour paints

A|In principle, the fewer washes, or glazes, the better. The primary wash should be simple, establishing a tonal base, and each successive layer or brushstroke should be darker, working light to dark. This way of building up colour is the principle method of working in watercolour. Of course, there are other techniques that can also be used, such as wet-on-wet and dry-brush (see Questions 35 and 37).

Three or four washes, or layers, of colour are often all that is needed to complete a painting, as watercolour is most effective in its simplicity. Too many colours laid over each other will lead to a muddied effect. To keep your painting under control, start with medium or large brushes, adding detail with smaller brushes if necessary.

Layering washes of the same colour can be used to suggest recession or changes in tone. Layers of different colours (or glazes, see Question 36), can be used to create tertiary colours.

A shoreline with distant cliffs offers a range of subtle tones for the watercolour painter. Here, I used simple glazes of colour to build soft gradations for the beach in the foreground, echoing the tonal layers for the background cliffs.

1 Lightly dampen the paper with a clean, moist sponge, applying more water at the top and less along the horizon. Leave a dry area in the middle of the sky to represent clouds. Mix a light wash from French ultramarine and ultramarine violet and apply it with a No. 8 squirrel brush. Add a touch of raw sienna to the clouds.

2 Mix a light wash of raw sienna and apply this to the foreground with the No. 8 brush. Mix a wash from sepia tone and sap green and work wet-on-wet over the raw sienna. Move the paint with dry and wet brushstrokes. Spatter the green mixture over the foreground to break up the flat tone. **Inset:** Using the No. 2 brush, apply a wash of ultramarine violet mixed with a little wash from Step 1, over the distant cliffs and along the horizon.

3 Mix a darker wash from ultramarine violet, viridian and burnt umber and overlay this on the distant cliffs. Leave a small gap at the top to give the impression of recession. As the washes dry, the different layers will be more clearly defined. Apply pure viridian along the shore. Add long streaks of colour with a dry brush on the foreground.

4 Use a warmer mix on the foreground from ultramarine violet, burnt umber and a little viridian. Use a dry brush to add broken texture to the strokes of colour along the shore. Once the painting is dry, the different layers are clearly visible.

The impression of the distant cliffs has been built up using just three layers of wash.

Texture is added to the foreground washes by pulling a dry brush across the image.

Q29 How do I stop the paint running?

A| A drip or run in the wrong place can be stopped with a tissue or brush, but once the drip has crept onto an area that is already painted, it will be very hard to remove and you may have to start again. Try not to overload your brush and keep your board relatively flat to avoid unwanted runs. Allow each layer of paint to dry before applying the next, unless you are working wet-on-wet, when runs and bleeds are a natural part of the painting process. Keep a supply of tissues, blotting paper or paper towels to hand to quickly lift-off runs before they dry.

Sometimes we want the paint to run! On a smooth, hot-pressed paper, the effects of wet colour can be used to good effect. Wet skies and clouds, for example, can be shown by applying a wet wash and tilting the paper.

A paper towel or piece of blotting paper may help to lift-off unwanted runs if applied quickly, but beware that the textured surface might mark the remaining wash.

Q30 How do I speed up drying time?

A| One of the pleasures derived from watercolour painting is its ability to slow down the mental process – waiting for washes to dry requires patience. However, there are a few ways of speeding up drying time, one is to use a hair dryer (not very practical on location), another is to add a few drops of alcohol to the water. One other solution is to work on two pictures in tandem, although this requires 'double' concentration!

When painting in the studio, you can use a small hairdryer to speed up the drying time. Hold it over a wet wash and move gently back and forth to avoid encouraging back runs in one spot.

TIP – Be aware of the paint spreading if you hold the hairdryer too close to the wash.

Chapter 3: Painting Techniques

Once you have mastered mixing colours and laying washes and glazes, you will be keen to extend your repertoire to include more detailed painting techniques. This chapter starts with the traditional watercolour methods of wet-on-wet and wet-on-dry, progressing to textural techniques such as dry-brush and spattering, how to use a sponge and resist techniques – invaluable for defining and maintaining highlights.

Q31 What is underdrawing?

A An underdrawing is a method of planning and sketching out the main elements of your composition before starting to paint. Use a soft 2B or 4B pencil to lightly indicate general shapes and areas. Remember that any pencil lines will be visible once the washes are applied, so keep them to a minimum and avoid shading. Using an eraser on watercolour paper can damage the surface, causing scuffing that will affect the adhesion of the paint. If you need to correct your drawing, use a soft kneaded eraser or resign yourself to starting afresh. On tinted or kraft paper, a soft sanguine Conté pencil is effective for underdrawing, but will smudge if too much water or wash is added over the top.

The rich colour of the sanguine pencil shows through the pale washes of body colour.

For this painting, I used a 2B pencil to draw the gate and the tree. I applied a pale wash on top, leaving the pencil to show through and define the details.

For this mixed media study on kraft paper, I used a sanguine Conté pencil to draw the outlines of the buildings, then applied opaque washes of colour to capture the mellow tones.

The contrast between the pure white of the gouache and the red of the pencil helps to define the shape of the figure.

Q32 What is underpainting?

A Underpainting is a technique where the initial outlines of the subject or composition are painted-in using a light, neutral tone. Always bear in mind that, due to the transparent nature of watercolour paint, these initial lines will show through any subsequent layers. This technique is ideally suited to working on location, when you want to get down all the elements of the scene in one sitting. This type of direct painting is sometimes referred to as alla prima (see Question 38). Think about the colour that you are going to use for the underpainting, as your initial brushstrokes will be an integral part of the finished image. You can start with a warm tone to capture the feel of a summer day, or use a blue that is a neutral shade, as in the project below, on to which you can build subsequent colours and areas of shadow.

Project

MATERIALS Arches rough paper 300lb (640gsm), No.5 round brush, watercolour paints

1 Ultramarine blue is a traditional colour to use for underpainting and particularly lends itself to landscape scenes. Mix a light wash of ultramarine blue and 'sketch' in the main elements of the composition, including shadows and a suggestion of the background sky.

2 Using a slightly darker wash of ultramarine blue, build the shadows and add further details to the building, indicating the tiles on roof.

3 Start to work on top of the underpainting, applying a light wash of burnt umber to the building, adding alizarin to the wash for the terracotta tiles on the roof. Mix a green from gamboge and ultramarine blue, and loosely indicate the meadow grass in the foreground. Using the underpainting as a guide, build on the shadow areas and add finer details to the building using darker washes.

The initial wash of blue shows through the subsequent washes to help to define the shadows.

4 Using the underpainting as a guide, build on the shadow areas and add finer details to the building using darker washes.

The loose brushstrokes of the underpainting give depth to the foreground.

Q33 What is wet-on-wet?

A The wet-on-wet technique gives the effect of colours bleeding and blending into each other, with softened edges and gentle feathering. It is achieved by applying paint or a wash to wet paper, or into a wet wash. You can blend washes of similar colours to achieve subtle tones, or apply one colour over another to create a third colour where the washes blend.

The extent to which the paint will run and blend will depend on the dampness of the paper. It is difficult to control the paint once it has been applied to wet paper, and soft, accidental effects can occur. For more control when using different colours, allow one colour to dry slightly before applying the next.

Paint applied by this method looks very different when dry, so try to avoid overworking the paint once it has been applied and allow the colours to move and merge to create some natural effects. Remember that the colours will appear lighter when dry.

The wet-on-wet technique is ideal for skies, sunsets, reflections, rain and mist but can be used for any subject where a soft, transitional effect is required.

Project

MATERIALS Smooth paper 140lb (300gsm), 3B pencil, No. 8 squirrel brush, No. 5 round brush, watercolour paints

The subtle variations in colour across a crab's shell can be captured with the wet-on-wet technique.

1 Using the 3B pencil, lightly draw the outline of the crab to establish the composition.

2 Mix a very pale wash from alizarin crimson and apply this onto dry paper, following the shape of the crab's body. Take the brush into the crenellated ridges of the shell and loosely suggest the position of the legs and claws. Add a little burnt sienna and sepia tone to the wash and dot it onto the paper allowing it to spread.

3 Strengthen the wash from Step 2 with more sepia tint and apply this to the curved top of the crab's shell. Add dashes of richer wash and allow the paint to bleed.

4 Wet the painting with a clean brush, taking care not to lift-off the paint. Apply dots of cadmium orange into the wet areas and a mix of alizarin crimson and sepia tint for a deeper colour. Use dots of the darker tone for the speckled pattern on the shell.

5 With a fine No. 5 brush use the darker wash from Step 4 to define the edge of the shell and layer paint on the claws and legs. Use dots for the bristles on the legs. Apply neutral tint for the pincers. Add a light wash of Naples yellow on the pale areas and suggest the background with a wash of neutral tint.

Q34 What is blending?

A | Blending is a technique that mixes colours or tones on the paper to achieve a gradual, soft change from one area to another. The wet-on-wet technique (see Question 33) achieves some natural blending effects.

Soft, transitional tones of light and shade are essential for describing form, for example if you are painting a rounded object. Roundness can be suggested with the primary washes using a large brush and painting the object darker on one side, with a wet-on-wet wash. Leave to dry then work into the shape with a smaller brush and darker wash. Try to avoid hard edges.

Blending medium slows drying time and is useful in hot climates where washes can dry almost instantly.

For this simple still life study, I used blending of two tones of green to describe the round form of the bowl. The subtle tones of the gourds were achieved by careful observation of the graduation from light to dark across the surface of the fruit. I worked the washes wet-on-wet to avoid any hard edges.

The subtle change in tone was achieved by blending tones wet-on-wet to follow the round shape of the gourd.

The soft transition from light to dark describes the round underside of the bowl.

Q35 What is wet-on-dry?

A This technique gives you more control over the paint than with a wash, to produce a painting with crisper lines and more defined edges to the colours. Traditional watercolour techniques rely on building up washes from light to dark, with the first underwashes being left to dry before applying the second and any tertiary washes or brushstrokes. Be aware that too many overlaid washes can create muddy colour. Studies of buildings or still lifes are suited to the wet-on-dry technique, as are paintings requiring tonal recession, such as mountains in distant landscapes, or the waves in a calm sea.

In this monochrome study, I pulled a dry brush across the paper to achieve a textured effect.

In this study, I painted wet-on-dry to describe the details of the tree branches and leaf fronds. I used a rigger brush for the leaves, using a relatively dry brush and building colour on the dry wash beneath.

The overlaid colours were applied onto dry underwashes to retain the edges of the shadows.

I used a small rigger brush to draw the feathery details of the leaves.

Q36 What is glazing?

A Glazing is a term often associated with oil paintings, where thin layers of paint are laid over one another in the early stages of a work. In watercolour, the term simply refers to laying one layer or wash of colour over another. Once the first wash is dry, a second wash is laid and the colours are built up. Watercolours are very transparent, with a few exceptions, and traditionally in watercolour painting, light colours are the first washes with two or three glazes added on top. You can either build up darker tones of the same colour using glazes, or overlay different colours, thus creating tertiary colours (see Question 15) with these superimpositions.

Below, the top row of illustrations show strong pigment superimposed with other colours. The three colours used are French ultramarine, aureolin and alizarin crimson. The bottom row shows the same colours with more water added to the washes, giving subtler tones.

This interior study uses glazes to build up the subtle tones within the arches. Three bands of overlaid colours define the foreground pews.

French Ultramarine

Aureolin

Alizarin Crimson

Q37 What is dry-brush technique?

A | Dry-brush involves applying paint or pigment to a dry paper surface to achieve some immediate and spontaneous textural effects. Use a dry brush dipped in a little undiluted paint and apply to paper with a rough surface using just one stroke for a textured effect, or to smooth paper for a cleaner, more solid line. You can continue to apply brushstrokes without replenishing the paint. To vary the density and texture of the line you can splay the bristles and drag the brush across the paper.

This technique is ideal for 'drawing' more linear details, such as furrowed fields, tree trunks or fence posts or for adding areas of texture, to a shingle beach for example.

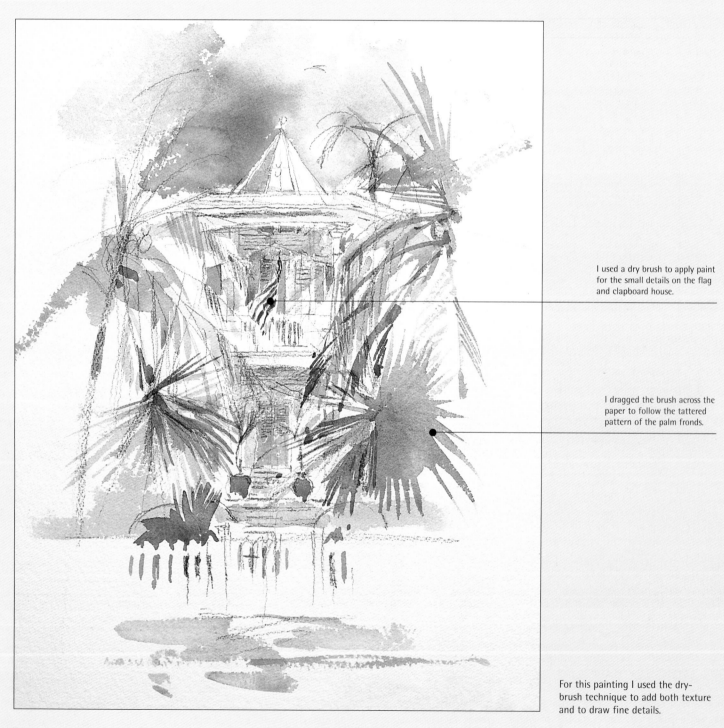

I used a dry brush to apply paint for the small details on the flag and clapboard house.

I dragged the brush across the paper to follow the tattered pattern of the palm fronds.

For this painting I used the dry-brush technique to add both texture and to draw fine details.

Q38 What is alla prima?

A Alla prima is a term often used in oil painting to describe a painting completed in a single layer of paint in one session. In watercolour, the principle is very similar, using limited washes applied direct to the paper without the use of an underdrawing. This method of direct, spontaneous painting suits subjects that are full of light as the transparent washes make the most of the luminosity of the paper. Working quickly like this, you will tend to use wet-on-wet techniques and achieve some unpredictable results. A limited palette (see Question 16) will also help you to work quickly, with the minimum number of washes.

This still life took approximately 20 minutes to paint. I worked straight onto the paper without any underdrawing, using simple brushstrokes to follow the shape of the trug and only two glazes of colour to define the shapes of the vegetables.

Two glazes of green have been used to describe the form of the marrow.

Accidental back runs often occur when working quickly with wet washes.

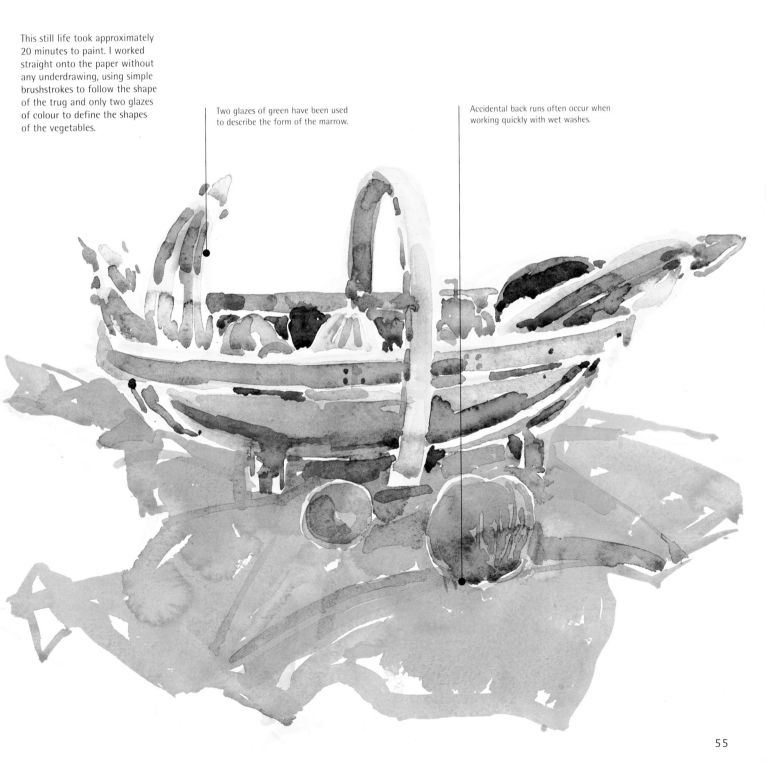

Q39 What is lifting out?

Project

MATERIALS   Bockingford rough paper 140lb (300gsm), sponge, No. 8 squirrel brush, kitchen paper, cotton bud, fine brush, watercolour paints

A | Occasionally you may need to remove paint for a particular sky or water effect. One method is to remove the colour from a wash while the paint is still wet. A sponge, tissue, cotton buds or a brush are all suitable for lifting out. Dab or lightly rub the paint until you have removed sufficient colour.

Your success may depend on the type of paper you use. A smooth paper, such as Bockingford, will respond well but a rough paper, such as Arches, tends to absorb the colour pigment more readily, making it hard to remove. Experiment on different papers before embarking on a painting where you wish to use this technique.

There is a transparent lifting preparation available which needs to be applied with a brush. When the preparation is dry, a wash is laid on top and when that has dried, the paint can be removed from the prepared area more easily. Bear in mind that some colours adhere to the paper more than others.

This technique is ideally suited to creating cloud effects. Using a damp piece of kitchen paper or tissue, you can lift out the sky colour to suggest soft, billowing clouds.

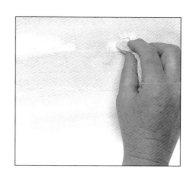

1 Mix a light wash of French ultramarine and lightly dampen the paper with a clean, moist sponge. Apply a gradated wash of blue for the sky area. Dampen a piece of kitchen towel or tissue and apply to the sky, rubbing gently to create a cloud shape.

2 Use a cotton bud for the more linear cloud shapes along the horizon. You can even use a clean, damp brush to 'draw' birds in flight.

The soft edges of these clouds were achieved by lifting off with a sponge.

A large area of wash can be removed with a damp piece of tissue to reveal the white of the paper beneath.

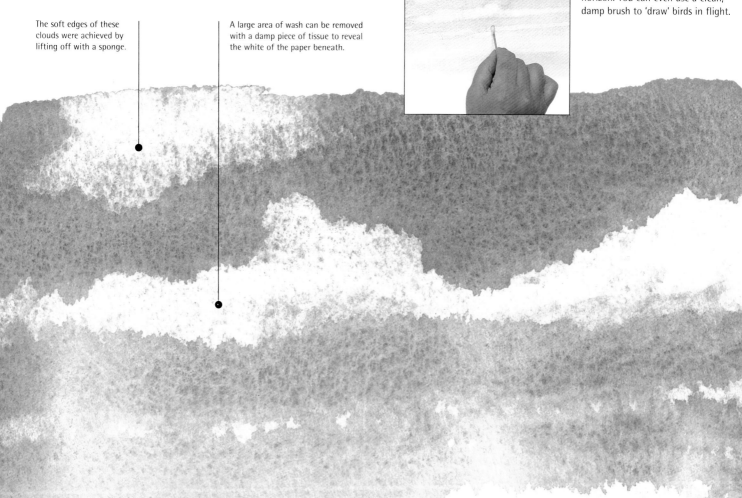

Q40 What is washing off?

A Sometimes mistakes are made and watercolour is a medium which, unlike oils, does not always respond well to corrections. You can, however, remove paint by washing off. Although this method does not remove the paint completely, you will be left with a sheet of paper gently toned by a blend of all the colours that you had used. Sometimes elements of your original composition remain, as some pigments are more permanent than others. You can incorporate these elements into a new picture or work on top of the old one.

Paint pigment has a high content of gum arabic, which sticks to the paper making washing off difficult. Some papers will wash or lift off a mistake better than others (see opposite). For example, Waterford responds well, but Arches, although a fine paper, will not respond to washing off with some colours. Experimentation is the key. Too much washing off will eventually damage the paper, losing its tooth.

Use a very damp sponge or large mop brush loaded with water to wash the colours together. The paper will buckle and will need to be restretched before you start a new painting. You can use a sponge or tissue to wipe off mistakes that are wet. You can also use this technique to create paint effects – lay a free area of pigment, let it dry, then immerse it in water or under the tap. Let it dry (or work on it wet) and stretch it.

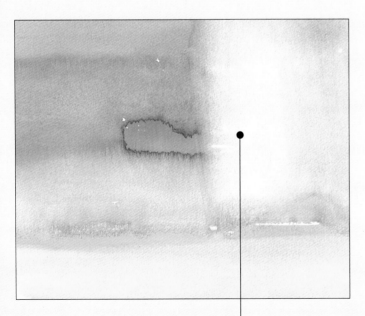

Here I have washed off an area of the damp wash where an unwanted back run occurred, using a damp sponge.

Q41 What is back run?

A This is a term used to describe areas of a wash that dry with a hard, uneven edge. They are sometimes called 'cauliflowers' or 'blooms'. They often occur unintentionally and can be welcome or unwelcome depending on the progress of your painting.

Back runs happen when a second wash is laid over a primary wash which is still damp, leaving an unwanted blotchy patch. Smooth, hot-pressed papers in particular encourage blooms more frequently. You can plan back run areas as part of the painting, using them to represent trees in full leaf, plant forms and skies. If an unwanted back run occurs, washing off is the only answer (see Question 40).

1 Dampen the paper and apply a flat wash of colour. Mix a darker wash and apply this immediately to the damp paper, dotting the colour onto the paper.

2 Leave the paint to spread. As the paint dries, a darker, feathered edge will appear.

In this study from my sketchbook, several accidental back runs have occurred, which add to, rather than detract, from the subject.

Q42 What is distressing?

A Both distressing and sgraffito (see right), are methods of making textural marks onto a watercolour painting **by removing certain areas of colour.** Distressing refers to rubbing with a flat blade or fine sandpaper onto dry colour. Use sandpaper with caution and try it on a spare piece of paper first.

1 Lay a light wash of warm ochre for the sky. Mix some of the sky wash with a little sap green for the foreground trees and shrubs. Allow the paint to dry completely. With a small piece of sandpaper gently rub an area of the sky in a circular motion to represent the setting sun.

2 Gently blow away any dust from the paper or lift-off with a soft kneaded eraser. The effect is of hazy, late-afternoon sun.

A small piece of fine sandpaper is perfect for gently rubbing away surface paint to create textural effects.

Q43 What is sgraffito?

A Sgraffito, from the Italian word for 'scratching', is the method of scraping away paint using a sharp blade **or scalpel.** You will need to work on a good, heavyweight rough paper, as the surface of a thin paper will tear. Remember that the washes must be completely dry before you start. Sgraffito can be used to represent driving rain, long grasses or foliage, or strands of hair.

I used a scalpel to draw hatched lines through the washes in the foreground of this painting. The sgraffito marks add texture and interest.

Q44 What is broken colour?

A The impressionist painters Georges Seurat (1859–1891) and Paul Signac (1863–1935) developed broken colour effects by juxtaposing dots of pure colour on the picture surface. When viewed from a distance, the colours merge in the viewer's eye, giving sparkle and luminosity. For extra contrast, juxtapose complementary colours (see Question 15). Broken colour can also be achieved by the dry-brush technique (see Question 37), using one stroke of a wide flat brush with the minimum of pigment on rough paper.

Broken colour is ideal for portraying dappled light or the sparkles of light on rippled water.

The contrast between the bright yellow and blue in the foreground adds to the vibrancy and light in this painting, conveying a hot, sunny day.

I used the contrast between complementary colours blue and yellow to simplify this image, combining dots of similar hues and tones to build up colour.

Q45 What effects can be achieved with a sponge?

A | **Using a sponge to apply paint will add sparkle and texture.** You can use a sponge to lift off colour (see Question 39), make alterations or wash off colour, grade washes or to simply add surface texture. Natural or synthetic sponges, sponge brushes and rollers are available.

Too much water in the sponge will lose the textural marks. Mix your colour in a saucer or palette and dip the sponge in, testing the amount of pigment before applying to the surface. Random, mottled effects can be achieved, but use them with restraint and not as a substitute for a brush.

I used a natural sponge to portray the dimpled skin of the lemon, overlaying a darker wash wet-on-wet.

Q46 What is stippling?

A | **Stippling is a broken colour technique (see Question 44), also known as pointillism.** Small dots of colour are placed next to each other to follow the form and pattern of the subject. By juxtaposing colours and varying the density of the dots you can create areas of light and shade, tone and depth. It is suited to flower and plant studies, sunny landscapes and textural architectural detail.

Stippling is best achieved with a round-ended brush, held vertically and dipped into a premixed wash. To complete a whole painting using this method would be painstaking, but it is quite effective in small areas. Cotton buds can also be used to give soft, round marks. An alternative method, although a little more random, is to apply some colour to a scrap of rough watercolour paper and, while still wet, press it onto a dry area of colour.

I used the end of a round brush to apply regular dots of colour to this simple study of a sunflower. Speckled, regular patterns often occur in nature and stippling is an ideal technique for more controlled patterns, compared to the random marks produced by spattering.

Q47 What is spattering?

A| Spattering is another method of adding lively texture to a picture, with random splashes and speckles of paint. Spatters can be applied in a variety of ways, but it is essential to mask off or protects areas where spatters would be unwanted.

One method is to tap a loaded brush onto a selected area either using your finger or with another brush. You can also use a toothbrush dipped into a mixed wash, then rub the bristles towards you with a match stick or your thumb. Spattering can be applied wet-on-wet into a wash, but be prepared for the marks to spread and perhaps disperse completely. For clearer effects work wet-on-dry. You can also spatter with masking fluid (liquid latex) before applying a wash (see Question 53).

Use spattering for the pebbles on a beach, close-ups of seed heads and grasses, speckles on fruit and flowers, and the pattern of an animal's fur or skin.

For this landscape, I applied spatters of paint in the middle distance to represent the irregular pattern of the hillside trees.

I spattered masking fluid across the foreground before applying any washes. Once the painting had dried, I removed the masking fluid to reveal the random speckles. I then added pure dots of red and yellow onto the spots of white, to represent the meadow flowers.

Q48 How do I add texture to a wash?

A | In addition to creating texture by distressing or spattering, you can make use of some natural effects to create a textured wash. Your first consideration should be the type of paper, as a rough paper will hold more pigment in the pitted surface. You can also exploit the natural granulation of some paint pigments – French ultramarine and burnt sienna, for example, leave tiny spots of pigment that coagulate as they dry, especially if undiluted.

Another natural, chemical reaction that can work to the artist's advantage is the effect of salt crystals – sprinkled over a wet wash they give an interesting, if random, texture. The salt will evaporate slowly and, when dry, it can be brushed off to leave flower-shaped, starburst marks. This technique can be applied to foreground detail, fabric textures or rock formations.

There are many additives available if you wish to experiment further. Gum arabic or glycerine added to a palette of pigment, or even a drop of honey, will thicken the mix enabling texture to be added with sgraffito techniques (see Question 43). These mediums will also slow down the drying time. Other mediums are available from art stores, such as granulation medium, texture medium and blending medium.

Rough paper holds the paint pigment in the surface.

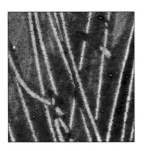

This effect was created by applying gum arabic to the wash and then drawing through it with the end of a brush to create raised lines.

This example shows the effect of texture medium added to a wash of colour.

This combination of granulation medium and cobalt creates a granulated effect in the wash.

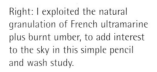

Right: I exploited the natural granulation of French ultramarine plus burnt umber, to add interest to the sky in this simple pencil and wash study.

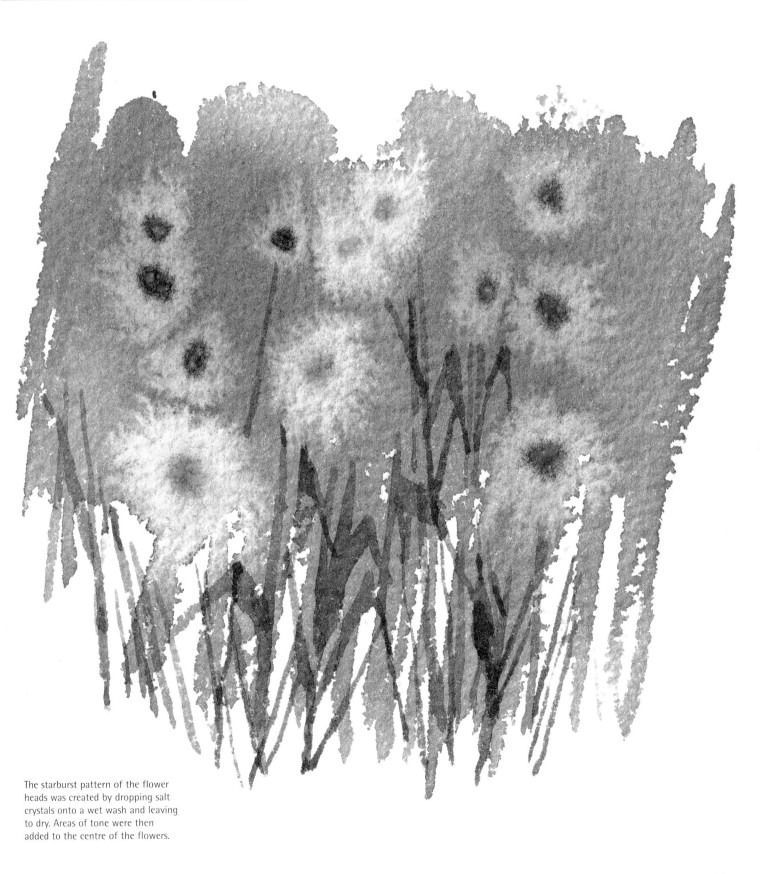

The starburst pattern of the flower heads was created by dropping salt crystals onto a wet wash and leaving to dry. Areas of tone were then added to the centre of the flowers.

Q49 What other media can be used in watercolour?

A | Watercolour painting has no hard and fast rules and through experimentation you will discover and develop your own style. A variety of media and techniques can be combined with watercolour to produce exciting and different effects.

Try using resist techniques (see Question 53) or overdrawing (see Question 50). You can combine watercolour with oil pastel for vibrant colours and textures. Acrylic is a water-based paint that can be used to tone a background. Water-soluble pencils work well with broad watercolour washes. Plaka is a casein emulsion-based water paint which is very opaque and completely waterproof when dry. Gouache can be mixed to give opacity (see Question 55).

This painting combines an initial drawing of oil pastel with a wash of watercolour on top. The oil pastel creates a resist effect.

I combined pencil and wash for this painting. The pencil underdrawing was used to define the balcony railings and details on the distant building.

Q50 What is overdrawing?

A Overdrawing is a painting effect that can be achieved with many different types of drawing medium. It is simply applying a drawing over the top of a watercolour painting. Pencils, dip pens, fibre tip pens can all be used. Pen lines can harden the soft edges of watercolour too much, so think twice before using ink. Some media may smudge when applied over a wet wash, use a very soft pencil to prevent smudging.

An ideal combination is watercolour pencils and watercolour wash. In this way you can combine colours and blend them into the background wash, either using a wet brush or wetted finger (see Question 11).

I started this painting by outlining the buildings and foreground harbour with a light underdrawing. I added washes of colour on top and then reinforced the details with a black 8B pencil.

The architectural details of the rooftops and windows are clearly defined by overdrawing with a black pencil.

The texture on the pebble beach is enhanced by overdrawing with pencil marks.

Q51 What is brush-ruling?

A| This is a technique that has only occasional use but can be helpful if you do not have a steady hand.
By using a ruler to guide the brush, you can paint a straight line across your picture. Brush-ruling is suited to architectural paintings where strong horizontals and verticals are required, or where the pattern of brickwork needs a regular line. You may wish to use it to represent the regular pattern of waves in a calm sea or for a painting which has a tighter, more controlled feel. This technique works best when applied wet-on-dry.

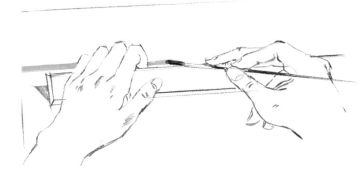

Hold the ruler raised slightly at an angle, using it to guide the brush which is kept on the edge by the middle finger.

The long 'racing eight' rowing boats, shallow steps and boathouse all lent themselves to the brush-ruling technique in this painting. A pattern of such regular lines is rarely seen in nature, but urban scenes offer more scope for experimentation.

Q52 How do I leave white areas in a wash?

A | **Watercolour is a very direct medium with freshness and purity.** It is a painting style that requires a certain amount of dexterity and spontaneity with the brush, and demands some practise and experimentation in order to control the paint and make use of the white of the paper. Leaving white areas in a wash will create a lively immediacy which can only be achieved with a larger sized brush, and relies on having plenty of premixed wash. Knowing when to stop is the key. Try to use the minimum number of strokes, as 'dabbing' will create fussy areas.

However, working quickly can occasionally cause problems. For example, if you leave an unintentional white area in a flat blue sky wash, it will be difficult to remove or paint over later. Plan your painting as much as possible before you start, using an underdrawing to outline the main elements of the composition or by leaving a dry area when damping the paper before laying a wash.

For detailed areas of white, such as window panes or a textile pattern, it is best to use a resist technique (see Question 53).

I carefully planned the progression of this painting to maintain the white of the paper to define the snow on the distant hills, the white-washed farmhouse and the fenceposts leading the eye into the picture.

The fine details of the roof, windows and house were painted wet-on-dry using a small brush with a good point.

The fenceposts were carefully painted around when applying the foreground wash.

The white snow on the distant hills was painted around when the washes of colour were applied.

Q53 What are resist techniques?

A| Traditional watercolour painting relies on the transparent quality of the pigment and the white of the paper to give translucency. The white of the paper is often the only highlight and its shape can be difficult to control, especially if you are working wet-on-wet. You can employ several techniques in order to ensure that the white paper retains its colour and shape.

Masking fluid is a liquid latex that can be painted or spattered onto a picture to define the white of the paper underneath. A wash is added over the top and, when dry, the masking fluid is rubbed away to reveal the white paper beneath. A recent product called permanent masking fluid is a non-removal fluid that can be useful for painting detail and for larger areas. It can be mixed with watercolour first.

Low adhesion masking tape is invaluable for adding a straight edge to the border of a painting, or for defining linear objects. Simply apply the tape to the paper and paint over the top. Once the wash is dry, the tape can be removed to reveal clean lines and edges.

Wax or oil pastel exploit the natural antipathy of grease and water for some interesting effects. They cannot be removed and should be used as part of your painting. Draw the shape of your subject with a wax crayon or oil pastel, or a candle if you wish the line to remain white, and then apply the watercolour paint over the top. The pastel or candle marks will repel the water.

I used several resist techniques in this moody, monochrome study. The windows of the distant cottage were drawn with masking fluid, while the rough textures of the foreground rocks were achieved by first applying strokes of candle wax to the paper. I used sea salt crystals to add texture.

Project

MATERIALS   Arches rough paper 140lb (300gsm), HB pencil, masking tape, masking fluid, reed pen, candle, small squirrel brush, No. 8 round brush, watercolour paints

This project combines several different resist techniques – masking tape to define the shadowed tones of the window panes, masking fluid for the flowers and candle wax for the mottled effect of the terracotta trough.

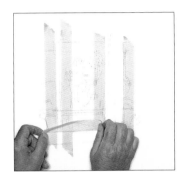

1 Lightly sketch the composition using an HB pencil. Mask off the dark shadows of the window pane with strips of masking tape and trim off the excess in order to follow the shape of the windows.

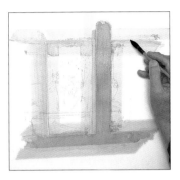

2 Lay a pale wash of neutral tint and Payne's grey along the edges of the window. Mask off the lighter areas of the recesses of the window panes, then apply a darker wash. Allow to dry thoroughly before removing the masking tape.

3 Apply the masking fluid with a reed pen, 'drawing' the shapes of the geranium flowers. For the delicate gypsophila flowers, tap the reed pen over the paper to spatter the masking fluid in a random pattern. Remember to cover any areas that you wish to keep clear of spatters. **Inset:** Shape the candle to a point, then rub across the plant trough to represent the mottled pattern of the stone.

4 Mix a light yellow-green wash from cadmium lemon and gamboge, and apply this to the background. For a richer, leaf green mix gamboge, cobalt and burnt umber and work wet-on-wet for the foreground foliage, adding the darks early.

5 Mix light red, raw sienna and burnt sienna for the terracotta trough, with touches of light red mixed with sepia added wet-on-wet. The candle wax will repel the paint to reveal a subtle mottling effect.

6 Mix a leaf green from raw sienna, cadmium lemon and cobalt and build up the pattern of the leaves. Use the negative shapes between the stems to help you establish the tracery of the foliage. Add touches of may green for the brighter leaves. Allow the paint to dry before gently rubbing away the masking fluid on the flowers.

7 Mix a rich wash of pure cadmium red with a touch of cadmium orange for the geranium flowers. Paint onto the white paper revealed by the masking fluid, this keeps the colours bright and zingy. Deepen the mix with a touch of alizarin crimson and apply this to the flower buds. You can strengthen the mix further by adding a touch of concentrated watercolour in rose.

Q54 How do I make colours appear more luminous?

A | Luminosity comes from using clean colour and the white of the paper. Paper is available in varieties of whiteness. A really white paper will produce more luminosity but will suffer from deterioration in time. Handmade paper, which is often 'acid-free', is preferable, although it is more expensive.

Colours have natural relationships to each other that can be exploited to enhance their effects. The juxtaposition of complementary colours (see Question 15), will give the colours more vibrancy and luminosity. Eighteenth- and nineteenth-century painters often used the device of a splash of red onto cool greens to give life to an area of a painting.

Concentrated watercolours (see Question 9) will give luminosity but will fade, as will most watercolour, should they be left in strong light for any length of time. One of the qualities of watercolour is its soft, subtle effects and too much luminosity can lose that subtlety.

Egg tempera is one of the oldest mediums in fine art. Used for many centuries for frescoes and icons, it is applied in several thin layers, mixed with water it will give pure transparent colour. The medium will need some study but ready-mixed egg tempera is available for experimenting. An iridescent medium is also available which will give a 'pearlescent' effect, it can be mixed with watercolour or applied over a previous laid wash. However, this medium will have limited appeal to traditional painters.

I painted this exotic still life in Morocco, using strong washes of gamboge and aureolin for the bright yellow cloth, with alizarin and raw sienna for the warm, terracotta fruit bowl. By painting alla prima with almost pure colour, I have captured the light and vibrancy of the subject.

Q55 How do I achieve an opaque effect?

A | Traditional watercolour methods rely on the transparency of the medium to layer and blend colours, working from light to dark. However, there may be occasions when you may wish to add opaque, light highlights to your work and this can be achieved by the addition of gouache (see Question 10), such as Chinese white, to a mix or directly onto the painting. Do not add gouache directly to pan watercolour as it will ruin the transparency of the colour.

'Plaka' casein colour is a type of emulsion paint, that is water-soluble and, when dry, is waterproof with a velvety finish. Light colours can then be applied over the dark colour when dry.

Opaque effects are suitable for figure studies, where you may wish to add highlights or mix paler washes for skin tones that can only be achieved by the addition of white.

This graphic still life is painted with plaka, a range of paints that are water-soluble but that dry with a matt effect.

The lighter highlights were applied over the dry waterproof colour of the underwash.

Project

MATERIALS Tinted handmade paper 200lb (425gsm), sanguine Conté pencil, Chinese white gouache, watercolour paints

Figure studies can be ideal subjects for using gouache. Skin tones can be built up from dark to light and the soft, subtle effects are ideally suited to nudes.

1 Lightly sketch the figure using a sanguine Conté pencil – the warmth of the colour on the tinted paper will enhance the skin tones. Mix a light wash of terre verte and apply this to establish the highlights.

2 Mix light red, yellow ochre and Chinese white gouache for a warm tone and apply to the upper arms and as a thinner wash to the legs. Mix yellow ochre and Chinese white for the hair and add dashes of pure white for the highlights on top of the shoulder, the elbow and the base of the back.

3 Continue to build darker tones on the arm. Using the mix for hair from Step 2, paint in the loose strands.

4 Continue to search for the highlights, adding details to the face and eyes. To put the figure in context, mix a dark wash of burnt umber and apply around the figure.

Q56 How do I correct an area of a painting?

A Gum arabic is one of the constituent ingredients of watercolour, it helps to bind the colour and also adheres to the paper, making it difficult to remove or 'lift' the paint, and hence making corrections virtually impossible once the paint has dried. Another factor to consider is the type of paper. Some good quality papers will take scratching away with a scalpel, some lighter weight papers will scuff or tear. Whichever paper you use, the wash or paint must be dry before your start to correct.

Rather than keep overworking a piece of watercolour, it is better to resign yourself to starting again with a new picture. Unwanted back runs (see Question 41) can be removed on some papers by carefully wiping with a sponge or tissue and then the wash re-laid once the paper is dry. You can correct work with a brush and clean water, but this will take time and patience.

Correcting details should be avoided, but a dark wash can be adjusted by lifting out with a damp sponge (see Question 39) or by scratching back with a scalpel.

You can remove a mistake or unwanted area of a painting by gently scraping away the dried wash with a scalpel. A heavy NOT or rough paper is best-suited to this technique, but take care not to remove too much of the paper surface if you want to add a wash over the corrected area.

Chapter 4: Watercolour Subjects

Watercolour lends itself to the subtleties of skies, seas and landscapes but it is equally as effective for still life and figure studies. Starting with a little background information on the principles of composition, perspective and lighting, this chapter explores different subjects, giving you advice on which techniques are best suited to particular situations – from a vase of flowers to a sleeping cat, or a stormy sea to a child's portrait.

Q57 How do I compose a painting?

A | An awareness of composition is essential in creating harmony in a picture and holding the viewer's interest. Once you have found the subject or theme for your picture, you will need to consider a number of factors before starting to paint. Choose a format, either landscape, portrait or square. The landscape, or horizontal, format is suited to wide views, allowing the eye to move from one side to the other, and is suited to open vistas. The portrait, or vertical, format is tall and encourages the eye to move up through the picture – it is suited to portrait studies or still lifes, and landscapes with vertical subjects. The square format is very contained, concentrating the eye on the centre of the image – it is suited to more detailed studies and close-ups. A small, neutral-toned card viewfinder will help you to select your format and chosen subject, and is especially useful in the wide vista of a landscape.

Make a series of thumbnail sketches to help you to focus on the main elements of the image. Thumbnails are simple drawings that explore different compositional options, whether different formats, crops, analyzing tonal contrasts or trying different arrangements in a still life, for example. To help you to analyze the picture space further, try dividing the picture into a grid of thirds. Placing the main elements of the composition, and the horizon line in landscape paintings, on the intersections of the grid will give a focus and help you to achieve a balanced and satisfying composition. Feel free to select elements from your scene, whilst leaving others out. You can always move things around to suit your composition, as long as you keep the lighting consistent.

You can also use some subtle devices to help lead the viewer's eye into the picture to the main focal points. Diagonal lead-in lines starting from the edge of the picture will direct the eye, for example a road or river in a landscape painting, or a linear object in a still life, can be used in this way. Use colour to draw the eye – a bright highlight or splash of complementary red in a green landscape will attract the viewer's attention.

In addition to exploiting these compositional devices, your choice of colour and the tonal arrangements within the picture space are also important in bringing a picture to life. Make use of complementary colours and the contrasts of colour temperature to emphasize or subdue your subject. You can also exploit the effects of light and shade in your composition. This is particularly effective in figure studies and still lifes where you can select the direction of light and the contrasts of light and shade (see Question 63).

This landscape view contains the whole facade of the building, compared to the close-up, portrait format, below right.

This sheet of paper shows some preliminary sketches and thumbnails in different formats – landscape, portrait and square. I often test my colours on the edge of the paper and this can be a useful way of recording particular colour mixes for future reference.

The shaded path and receding arbour of vines, draw the eye into the picture toward the sunlit focal point in the background, placed at an intersection of thirds.

Seated figure studies generally suit a portrait format. The model's legs create an undulating line that lead the eye into the picture area.

This still life uses the lobster's pincers as diagonal lead-in lines, forming a pleasing triangular composition.

Q58 What size should my painting be?

A | Once you have decided upon your subject matter and composition, you may be unsure at what scale to render your painting. The decision is really quite a personal one but can be governed by the subject matter, your painting style, the amount of time you have available and the size of your paper.

Some subjects lend themselves to large scale paintings – seascapes, skyscapes and landscapes call for broad washes that work well over a larger area. Still lifes and close-up studies are more suited to a smaller scale where you can add finer detail. But, of course, a small, intimate sketchbook study of a beach scene or landscape is equally effective.

The sizes of watercolour paper vary enormously and this may be a deciding factor. Paper can be bought by the roll and some sheets are available that measure 1524 x 1219mm (60 x 48in). A piece of handmade, mould made or machine made paper 560 x 760mm (22 x 30in) is manageable, and cut into two or four makes it easier to use still. Small sketchbooks are invaluable for outdoor work. However, working on a small scale for finished pictures can often make the work too busy.

This landscape painting measures 560 x 760mm (22 x 30in). Painting on such a scale allowed me to use a large brush for the sky wash and for the details in the foreground.

I painted this study in a small sketchbook, giving it an intimate mood and using a limited palette of colours with loose brushstrokes.

Q59 What is squaring or gridding up?

A| This technique illustrates the value of keeping a sketchbook with you at all times. A small drawing or watercolour sketch can be enlarged into a finished picture. Start by dividing the smaller drawing or sketch into equidistant squares by overlaying a light pencil grid, then label them with numbers or letters. Select the size of your finished picture and divide the area into squares of the same proportion. The smaller sketch can now be plotted to the larger format. Transfer the main elements of the composition and do not include too much detail.

Early portrait painters used a wooden frame, divided by thread and fixed to their easel, through which to view their subject. Their canvases were marked with proportionate squares. The subject was viewed through the grid and their features plotted onto the canvas. For this method to be successful you must maintain your position, as a slight shift can result in a totally different viewpoint. Small plastic viewfinder grids are now available in art stores that achieve the same result if held at arm's length.

1 Using a 3B pencil, lightly draw a grid of 30mm (1¼ in) squares over your chosen watercolour sketch. Label the axes.

2 On a larger piece of paper, draw a grid one and a half times larger, using 45mm (1¾ in) squares and label the axes to match the smaller grid. Plot the main elements of the sketch using the grid marks as a guide, for example D4.

Q60 What are negative shapes?

A| When drawing or painting you need to be observant. Negative shapes in a painting or drawing are the spaces 'in between' the positive subject. Being aware of these spaces helps you to paint accurately and they are very important, both in the construction and composition of a piece of work. Simple objects, such as a chair, table or a still life, will all have negative shapes in between the solid, positive shapes of the objects themselves. You can find negative shapes in a landscape between the trunks and branches of trees, for example.

In figure drawing, the composition and sense of harmony and form will be made more obvious with the search for the 'negatives'. For example, by searching for the triangular space created in the crook of an elbow, you will accurately render the shape of the arm.

I rendered the complex pattern of branches by using the negative shapes in between to define their outlines.

This simplified example highlights the negative shapes of the blue background seen though the tree's branches.

Q61 What is perspective?

A Perspective is defined as the art of drawing or painting solid objects on a two-dimensional surface, giving a three-dimensional appearance. There are many complex rules to perspective that need not really concern the artist. In order to paint perspective with accuracy, you need only remember two simple principles: parallel lines appear to converge at a point on the horizon and objects appear smaller and narrower as they recede into the distance. These principles are known as linear perspective. A sense of depth can also be achieved by a principle known as aerial perspective (see opposite) that exploits contrasts of colour, tone and texture to convey distance.

Linear perspective can be illustrated by imagining a straight path or railway track. In the far distance the parallel sides of the track will converge at a point on the horizon. This is known as the vanishing point. Perspective lines above the horizon will appear to slant down and those below the horizon will slant up. The horizon line is located at eye level (see Figure 1). This is one-point linear perspective.

The side of a cube, or house for example, viewed straight on will not change shape. However, if viewed from the corner a principle known as two-point perspective comes in to play. The two parallel sides of the house will diminish toward separate vanishing points (see Figure 2). Three-point perspective applies to tall objects or buildings when viewed from below. The lines will diminish toward a vanishing point above the object (see Figure 3).

Perspective can also be found in figure drawing and still life painting, known as foreshortening. This applies where a long narrow object, a leg for example, appears narrower and shorter as it recedes into the background. Circles are also affected by perspective, becoming ellipses.

In this painting, the road slopes upwards. An 'auxiliary' vanishing point above the horizon line will be introduced to determine the slope of the road.

Figure 1 – One-point perspective
The parallel sides of the road appear to converge at a point on the horizon, the vanishing point.

Figure 2 – Two-point perspective
The parallel edges of the two house walls converge toward separate vanishing points on the horizon.

Figure 3 – Three-point perspective
The vertical edges of the tower walls will eventually converge at a vanishing point in the sky.

TIP – A very simple aid to judge the angle of an object or a perspective line is to cut two pieces of card approximately 2.5 x 20cm (1 x 8in) in length, joined at the top by a paper fastener to create 'scissors'. Hold the scissors with one arm of the 'L' against a perpendicular and then move the other arm to line up with the perspective angle.

Q62 What is aerial perspective?

A Aerial perspective, or atmospheric perspective, is an artistic principle that is used in landscape paintings to convey distance and atmosphere. It is most clearly seen in wide, panoramic views where distant hills or fields can be viewed on the horizon through a haze. You can convey this effect through the use of colour, tone, texture and scale.

Colour temperature is very effective in creating a sense of distance. Warm colours advance and cool colours recede. Use warm colours, such as reds, browns and yellows, in the foreground and cooler blues, violets and greys for the distant hills along the horizon.

Gradations of tone also give a sense of depth. Work from light to dark, with the lightest tones along the horizon, using layers of washes to build the depth of tone into the foreground.

Texture and detail will lift a painting. Use finer detail in the foreground with strong colour and tone, with softer and more abstract shapes in the far distance with a blue, hazy cast.

Scale is another useful device. Objects in the distance are smaller than those in the foreground. You can apply this to skies by layering clouds, with smaller, paler clouds in the distance.

Of course, atmosphere can change the colour we see: a sharp, clear day will differ from a hot, hazy day; late evening clouds add another dimension of colour, introducing blues, mauves and greys. One way of seeing these changes of colour and tone is to try to view the subject upside down by tilting your head.

The soft blue tone of the hills is carried forward into the middle ground to suggest a haze.

A distant panorama will reveal a cool, hazy horizon that typifies the characteristics of aerial perspective. Use layers of cool tones for distant hills, contrasted with warmer hues in the foreground.

Q63 How do I light a subject?

A In any form of painting, lights, halftones and darks are essential for conveying form. You can affect the mood and composition of your painting by controlling the light and shade that define your subject. Natural light is preferable for painting but you will need to work quickly as the cast shadows will obviously change as the sun moves. Alternatively, you can use artificial light in a number of different positions to achieve a variety of effects.

A side lit subject will cast long shadows to one side. The side that is lit will be bright with strong highlights, in dramatic contrast to the shadowed side. A top lit subject will throw a short shadow beneath, with highlights on the top. A backlit subject, or *contre-jour*, will appear mainly in shadow, with soft diffuse detail, almost creating a silhouette with halos of light.

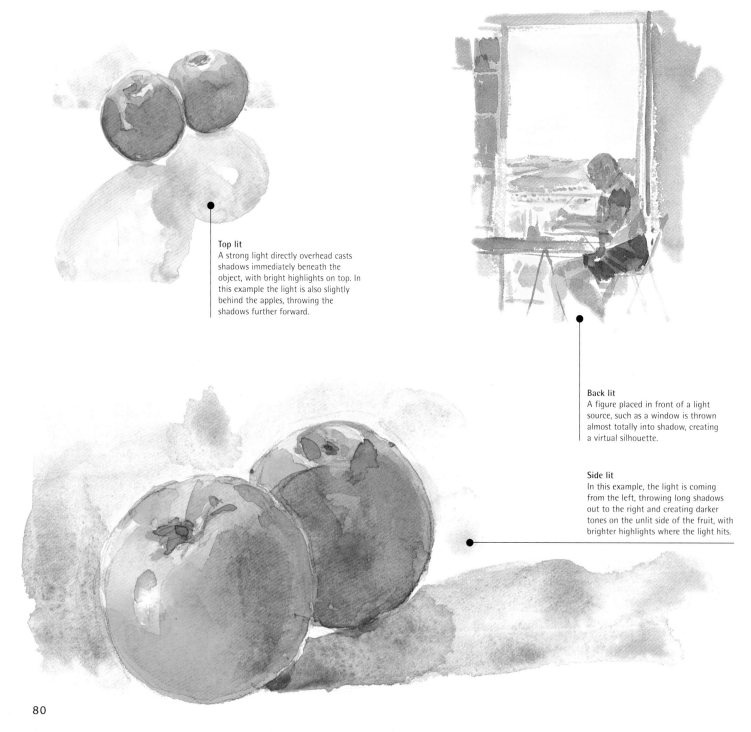

Top lit
A strong light directly overhead casts shadows immediately beneath the object, with bright highlights on top. In this example the light is also slightly behind the apples, throwing the shadows further forward.

Back lit
A figure placed in front of a light source, such as a window is thrown almost totally into shadow, creating a virtual silhouette.

Side lit
In this example, the light is coming from the left, throwing long shadows out to the right and creating darker tones on the unlit side of the fruit, with brighter highlights where the light hits.

Q64 How do I paint light and shade?

A | The play of light across a landscape can often be the inspiration behind your painting, whether it be the dramatic contrasts of light and shade, the subtle effects of dappled light or an overall luminosity. Watercolour is the perfect medium for capturing the effects of light.

Before you start your painting, you need to assess the direction and intensity of the light. Making a monochrome, tonal sketch of the scene will help you to identify contrasts of light and shade and exploit them in your composition. Contrasts of tone work well in brightly lit landscapes.

Sometimes, the changes in tone are more subtle and the light appears more luminous. This type of light and shade, found in dappled sunlight through trees or on a hazy day, can be rendered using broken colour effects (see Question 44) or by using the wet-on-wet technique (see Question 33) to achieve soft transitions of colour and tone. Dappled sunlight under trees can be shown with a randomly applied wash, either wet-on-wet or wet-on-dry, over an existing lighter tone.

The intensity of the light will be affected by natural factors – the time of day, the season and the weather – and you should be aware of their different effects to render them accurately. All these factors will affect the colour temperature of the light: an early morning is generally cooler in tone than evening; a summer day is brighter than midwinter; rain clouds cast a cool shadow over a landscape. Shadows are an important element of any painting and will be discussed further in Question 68.

This monochrome study conveys bright, dappled sunlight. The white of the paper creates a stark contrast with the dappled shadows thrown onto the wall and the deep shadow seen through the open door establishes the darkest tone.

Project

MATERIALS Arches rough paper 140lb (300gsm), 4B pencil, No. 8 squirrel brush, No. 4 sable brush, watercolour paints

This monochrome painting uses Payne's grey, a colour named after the artist William Payne who founded a drawing school in 1790. His students were encouraged to look at light and shade and interpret the tonal values in monochrome before using a full palette.

1 Lightly pencil in the composition. Mix a small amount of paint with a palette of water to make a pale wash and apply to the background for the lightest tone.

2 Once the first wash has dried completely, mix a slightly darker wash using more pigment and less water. Apply this secondary wash to define the features in the foreground and to introduce some negative shapes.

3 Make a darker wash, adding detail to the roof and the areas of shadow in the windows and arch.

4 The final, darkest wash is used to 'draw' finer details in the grasses in the foreground, giving the painting depth.

Q65 How do I convey the time of day?

A | **The choice of colours in your palette will change from dawn to dusk.** Shadows will soften, harden and lengthen, and the sky will show a variety of changes in colour and mood. Early morning light is often a 'golden' time to paint, with long shadows and fresh light. At midday, colours are more burnt-out and with the sun directly overhead the shadows are shorter and their colour clearer. At dusk, the setting sun gives a warm glow and the shadows lengthen. A soft, washed out image of the sun in the morning or evening can often dramatize a sky.

A good exercise is to paint the same subject at different times of day – morning, midday, afternoon and evening – observing light and shadow colour changes. Painting outdoors will always be more comfortable in the early morning or evening, as working in the midday sun on to white paper can be a strain on the eyes unless protected by some shade, and you will have to work quickly, as the shape and position of the shadows will change as the sun moves. Indicate the shadows in a light pencil so that you can adjust their position as you work.

The top of the tree is lighter in contrast to the lower branches which are in shadow, reflecting the bright sunlight.

The cast shadows are intense and short, falling directly beneath the objects, conveying the time of day.

I painted this scene in late morning, as the sun was almost at its highest point. The colours are fresh and bright and the shadows short. I used a warm toned, handmade paper to establish the colour temperature.

Q66 How do I capture the qualities of evening light?

A | **In the evening, you will see muted tones with possibly silhouetted trees and buildings.** Shadows will lengthen and appear in the opposite direction to those in the morning and the overall tone will be warmer. The sky may show pink tones towards the horizon and the setting sun will reflect warm light on to the landscape. Your palette may range from warm yellows and reds to cool blues, cerulean, ultramarine violet and Payne's grey. Sunsets make attractive subjects for paintings (see Question 77).

Painting at night will require a different palette using a range of neutral greys. A moonlit landscape will appear in tones of dark green-blue.

I used a flat wash of yellow ochre to create an overall harmony across the sky.

The hazy, late evening sun was created by gently rubbing a piece of sandpaper in a circular motion.

The muted hues of late evening light softened the stark nature of this subject, making a pleasing study with a quiet, still mood.

Q67 How do I simulate bright sunlight?

A | In sunlit pictures, light and dark areas, together with strong shadows, should be prominent. Use the shape and intensity of the shadows to indicate the strength of the sun, keeping the colour of the objects that are in sunlight strong and rich, too. The midday sun is very bright and you can indicate this by making the most of the white of the paper. The introduction of cool, complementary colours will contrast and enhance the warm tones. A bright, cloudless blue sky combined with say, ochres, siennas and reds will immediately show the 'temperature' of a picture. Shadows are transparent, so do not use black, but look for the colour in shadows, often they pick up the colour on which they fall, so the transparency of a wash is important. Winter sunshine will also produce positive, long shadows often with a cooler palette of blues and greys.

A warm-toned watercolour paper immediately establishes a ground tone. Some papers may need the addition of opaque white for the highlights if they are of a darker tone. A sanguine Conté pencil used sparingly can be used for underdrawing, as the pencil marks will run into warm tones.

There are very few days in Morocco when there is no sunshine, this picture contrasts the white of the buildings with the bright reds and oranges on the carpets. I used a palette of cobalt blue for the sky, warm Naples yellow for a transparent wash over the paving, and ultramarine violet with a touch of burnt umber for the strong shadows.

A sense of bright sunlight can be conveyed by looking out onto a scene from the shadows. The warm light falling into this courtyard is emphasized by the contrast with the muted shadow in the foreground.

Q68 How do I paint shadows?

A | **Shadows are essential in any painting of light and shade, indicating the direction and intensity of light.**
To paint shadows effectively you need to look hard at the colours within them – shadows are never black but a muted version of the objects that they fall onto. The time of day also has an effect, as shadows will have different colour temperature values in the cool morning compared to the warmer tones of the evening. In intense light, the contrast between light and shadow is strong, shadows are clearly defined and the transition from one area to another is sharp. In hazy light, shadows are softer with less defined edges.

Shadows contain reflected colour – from the sky, from the object casting the shadow and from adjacent areas of local colour. Add touches of complementary colours to your shadows. Start with primary washes to establish the undercolour and tone, the second wash will need to determine the strength of the shadow colour. This wash can be applied wet-on-wet or wet-on-dry. A good 'shadow' mix is ultramarine violet with burnt umber. A shadow thrown across an area of light green might be a mix of Payne's grey, viridian and gamboge.

Sometimes all you need do to throw an area into shadow is to apply a cool colour wash over the top, or you may find that you simply need to darken your original wash to achieve a shadow tone. A common error is to mix too strong a colour, remember that you are painting the interaction of light (and shade). An interior will show the tone values of shadows, a white wall is never white against the strong light from a window.

Project

MATERIALS Arches rough paper 140lb (300gsm), sanguine Conté pencil, squirrel brush, No. 5 round brush, watercolour paints

The dappled light falling through the arbour of vines caught my eye. The intensity of the sunlight is conveyed through the short, dark shadows and the warmth of the surrounding tones.

1 Lightly sketch in the main elements of the composition using the sanguine Conté pencil. Search for the areas of light and shade and the tonal variations across the shadows. Apply a light wash of cerulean for the sky and place the shadows on the left-hand side.

2 Mix a light wash of aureolin and apply this over the blue for the areas of bright light and highlights. Mix a warm wash of Naples yellow with a touch of light red for the foreground. **Inset:** Mix delft blue and raw sienna and drop this wet-on-wet for the foliage, taking the colour around the light of the focal point at the end of the covered path.

3 Continue to build the tones on the tree on the right and establish the warm tones of the foreground with the mix from Step 2, working wet-on-dry. Drop in touches of shadow colour mixed from ultramarine violet under the vine arbour and tree, using a combination of wet-on-wet and wet-on-dry techniques.

4 Build up the tones in the shadows with ultramarine violet and burnt umber with a thin wash of colour that allows the underlying glazes to show through, giving the impression of dappled light. Start to delineate the main structures of the arbour and the building on the left, carrying the shadow colour into the recesses of the door and windows and building up the detail on the vines to give an impression of depth. Flick paint across the foreground to add texture.

5 Mix a dark brown from ultramarine violet and burnt umber for the tree trunks and a burnt sienna and neutral tone for the wooden supports and the vines. Add the shadow beneath the tree on the right to help to anchor it to the ground and give the impression of a high, intense sun.

Q69 How do I paint landscapes?

A Landscapes are, and always have been, a favourite subject for many artists. There are many ways of approaching landscape painting – you will need to consider the light, the inclusion of any buildings, the colours and tones of fields, hills and trees, and the sky conditions. The use of aerial perspective (see Question 62) will help you to convey distance in broad vistas.

Use a small sketchbook for preliminary sketches. Planning a picture will involve choosing a format, you can use a viewfinder to help you to select and crop your composition and help to clarify your ideas. Next, consider the balance of the image, whether the landscape will dominate the foreground, or whether the sky warrants more emphasis. Look for interesting patterns and shapes, perhaps a ploughed field or the various greens of a deciduous wood.

Far left: A landscape includes any subject outdoors. I was drawn to the greens of this view, using the formal urn to add interest to the foreground.

Left: This landscape includes several different elements: a rocky shore, a distant building, a glimpse of water and background hills, together with a summer sky.

I filled a double page of my sketchbook with this classic panoramic view. The variety of bright, sunny greens lead the eye through to the cool distance and into the light sky with drifting clouds.

Q70 How do I paint mountains?

A| **The drama of mountain scenery is a lure for many artists.** Select your format and composition carefully – a landscape format will emphasize the breadth of a mountain range, whereas a portrait format will accentuate the scale of a single peak.

You will need to consider the effects of aerial perspective (see Question 62) and perhaps exploit linear perspective (see Question 61), to follow a ridge into the distance. Plan your painting carefully to keep the white of the paper for any snow-capped peaks or crags, or use white gouache to add snowy details on a grey midtone paper.

Wet-on-wet techniques are very effective for conveying the misty heights of mountain peaks, combined with wet-on-dry brushstrokes for the finer details of rocky ridges and scree. Include a building or a figure to give your painting a sense of scale.

The buildings appear to be dwarfed by the mountain, adding to the sense of the scale.

I took colour from the mountain peak down into the water to help to link the picture together.

I chose a portrait format for this painting commissioned by the Scottish Tourist Board, emphasizing the great height of the mountain sides. I used the wet-on-wet technique for the blues of the rocky peak, using darker tones to shape the craggy, shadowed rock faces.

Q71 How do I paint trees and foliage?

A| **This question is frequently asked, but not easily answered.** There are so many species of trees and permutations of seasons, weather and scale. It is simpler to identify a few general tree shapes and to observe their overall structure from the skeleton of a bare trunk and branches in winter to the masses of foliage in midsummer. The most common shapes are rounded, conical, cylindrical and columnar. Use these general shapes to suggest woods in distant landscapes.

For closer studies you may wish to identify the various kinds of tree and their characteristics of shape and foliage. It can help to establish the character of a tree by making a study of a leaf, followed by a branch and then render the whole tree, based on its internal structure of trunk and branches.

The complicated pattern of bare branches and twigs can be accurately painted by observing the negative shapes between branches (see Question 60). To give form and solidity to a bare tree, blend darker tones on the shadowed side of the trunk or branch. For a tree in leaf, use the direction of light to show the third dimension, trees are usually darker on the lower branches, with shadows on the undersides of the leaf masses. Find a shorthand to express the massing of leaves rather than painting each one individually.

Use a rigger brush for the detail on branches, following the natural shape of the branch from base to tip with the brush. Some foliage, for example palm fronds, lends itself to a fan brush or the dry-brush technique.

For this close-up study of a small mulberry sapling, I mixed a variety of greens to define the shapes of the individual leaves, giving the impression of dappled light.

You can make a study of leaves or a branch to familiarize yourself with a tree's characteristics.

This magnificent cedar lent itself to a rigger brush. I worked wet-on-dry, using light brushstrokes, flicking the brush to follow the feathery shape of the foliage. The shadow beneath the tree helps to anchor it to the picture plane.

Project

MATERIALS Arches rough paper 140lb (300gsm), HB pencil, large squirrel brush, No. 8 round brush, watercolour paints

This project illustrates the range of shapes and colours that can be found in a green landscape. Foreground trees will show more detail in branches and leaves compared to the softer, rounded shapes and tones of distant woods.

1 Lightly sketch the outline of your composition with an HB pencil. Loosely shade the underside of the leaf masses to give form to the foreground tree and indicate the shadows.

2 Mix a light sky wash from cobalt blue and a touch of cerulean and take it across the sky and trees in the middle ground. Warm up the mix toward the horizon with a touch of raw sienna and light red. While the wash is still wet, add a mix of aureolin and raw sienna for the bright, lime green of the tree where the light falls and carry this colour onto the foreground grass.

3 Drop a mix of ultramarine, aureolin and burnt umber onto the tree to render the darker tone under the top branches and on the trees on the right, working wet-on-wet. Add a touch of ultramarine to the mix and apply to the distant trees, the cooler colour will enhance the sense of distance.

4 Continue to use the darker tones to establish the form of the foreground tree, an elm. Add suggestions of branches and leaf masses to the middle ground trees with short, upward brushstrokes using a No. 8 round brush.

5 Add details of the branches of the elm with burnt umber applied with the No. 8 round brush. Build up three washes on the trees and use dashes at the end of the branches to represent the leaves. Mix a darker blue-green wash for the distant trees and carry some of this colour into the foreground as a light shadow wash. Use a dry brush in the foreground.

Dry brushstrokes combined with spattering and long grasses add texture to the foreground.

Distant trees are represented by soft shapes in cooler hues.

Short, upward strokes follow the cylindrical shape of the poplars.

Q72 How do I paint autumnal scenes?

A| In the autumn, the landscape painter's palette will change. Trees will turn gold, vineyards red and orange, and fields soft ochres and browns. Trees will start to shed their leaves to reveal their skeletal form, enabling you to see the structure and shape more clearly. The sun throws longer shadows. All these elements will give an autumnal feel to your painting. To establish a warm midtone, work on a toned paper such as oatmeal, or tone the paper with a flat wash of raw umber.

A suggested palette for this time of year might include: cadmium red, light red, alizarin crimson, burnt and raw umber, and cadmium yellow together with cooler ultramarine violet for mixing and shadow areas. To practise mixing colours, collect fallen leaves and make simple studies.

The addition of warm ochres and browns gives the subtle impression of approaching autumn in this landscape.

Fallen leaves make perfect subjects for studies in colour and shape.

Q73 How do I convey the effects of rain and mist?

A| The weather is not always sunny, and painting a wet, rainy day is something worth trying. Of course, it is no fun to sit outside to paint and rain is a very unpredictable wet-on-wet technique that can adversely affect the washes on a picture. You may wish to take photographs and make notes and sketches before returning to the relative comfort of your studio or car to commence painting.

The weather is a great gauge of mood in a painting. A dark approaching storm, a misty winter's day, a moment caught of scudding rain clouds, or, from inside, looking through a window at a howling gale. All will have their own drama and characteristics. Wet cityscapes can inspire images of reflections in puddles, glistening pavements and multicoloured umbrellas.

The wet-on-wet technique is ideally suited to rain-laden skies, giving feathered effects of heavy clouds. By tilting the paper as you apply a wet wash, you can encourage the paint to run vertically, suggesting driving rain. Mist can be conveyed in a similar way, using wet-on-wet and blending to soften edges. Use a tissue to lift-off areas of a wash to suggest swirling mist coming over the top of a mountain, or hanging over a damp field on a winter's day.

The cold, damp atmosphere of a Welsh slate village is conveyed through the use of a grey tinted paper and neutral washes of colour, blending wet-on-wet to give the impression of mist on the distant hills and a damp road in the foreground.

I created this rain-laden sky by working wet-on-wet, allowing the passages of colour to merge.

Q74 How do I convey the effects of snow and ice?

A | Looking at a snowscape from your window can be a source of inspiration, whether you live in the city or country. Take as many notes and sketches as you can before the snow melts. When the sun shines on a snowscape we become aware of contrasting shades and colours which are unfamiliar. Blues, greys and browns are often the only colours that you will need in your palette. Colour can be heightened by contrasting cool colours against, for example, bright warm colours, perhaps of children's scarves and hats as they play in the snow.

When planning a snowy painting, use resist techniques (see Question 53) to mask out finer details, such as snow laden branches or roofs, and leave white areas in your wash for blankets of snow. Lift-off a light coloured wash from a mountain peak or use sandpaper to lightly rub away a snowy area (see Question 42). Snowscapes have a naturally cool feel, and you can suggest this by using a toned grey or blue paper combined with white gouache to add an opaque, snow effect. Spattering masking fluid or opaque paint onto the picture can by used to suggest flurries of snow.

I used the white of the paper to convey the layer of snow across this scene. By using the sky colour in the shadow mixes falling across the foreground, I gave the impression of the cold, bright light found on crisp, winter days.

I used white gouache to add the snow-capped peaks in the distance.

The grey-blue tinted paper sets the tone for this snow scene.

Q75 How do I paint skies?

A│ Skies, of course, can vary from day to day and often, minute by minute, and you will need to be well-prepared before you start if you are painting on location. Skies present myriad shapes and colours depending on the type of cloud formation, the light and time of day. You may wish to sketch the different cloud effects to familiarize yourself with their characteristics and decide on your painting technique. In any skyscape, the sky and land should relate to each other, with similar values of light. To help establish a link, lay a toned wash across both the sky and land at the start of the painting and use some of the sky colour in the landscape as you work. When planning a skyscape, consider the position of the horizon; a low horizon will give dominance to the sky, whereas a high horizon will create a more intimate sky.

To paint a cloudless summer sky, start with a single gradated wash, making it darker at the top and lighter towards the horizon, following the rules of aerial perspective (see Question 62). You could add a subtle hint of raw sienna along the horizon using the wet-on-wet technique.

Completely clear skies do not always stay that way for long and you will need to study the various cloud shapes in order to complete a skyscape (see Question 76).

This simple sky study, with low level clouds, was painted wet-on-wet using Payne's grey, indigo and raw sienna. The birds, and the vapour trail in the sky below, were created using sgraffito.

Here, the sky fades from a strong cobalt blue to a pale violet along the horizon, tinged with raw sienna. The white of the cumulus clouds was achieved by leaving the white of the paper to represent the tops.

The soft tones in this skyscape were created by subtle blends of wet-on-wet washes, using a very pale underlying wash and gentle gradations of colour, using ultramarine and a little Payne's grey.

This rain-laden sky with low stratus clouds is a mix of cobalt, cerulean, raw sienna and a touch of alizarin crimson. The colours were dropped wet-on-wet and left to blend naturally.

Project

MATERIALS Arches rough paper 140lb (300gsm), No. 8 squirrel brush, watercolour paints

You can achieve an effective sky study with a few simple washes.
'Draw' with the wash to use the white of the underlying paper
to represent clouds.

1 Float clean water onto the paper, leaving a few dry areas of white paper for the clouds. Mix a large wash of cobalt blue to make a fairly thin colour. Working quickly, build the wash around the top of the clouds, softening the edges slightly. **Inset:** Apply more of the wash in narrowing layers toward the horizon.

2 While still wet, mix a wash of either Naples yellow or raw sienna and apply just below the top of the clouds to represent the sun hitting the higher areas.

3 Mix a neutral shade from cobalt blue and alizarin crimson with a touch of burnt umber. Gently apply this to the wet areas underneath the clouds and along the horizon.

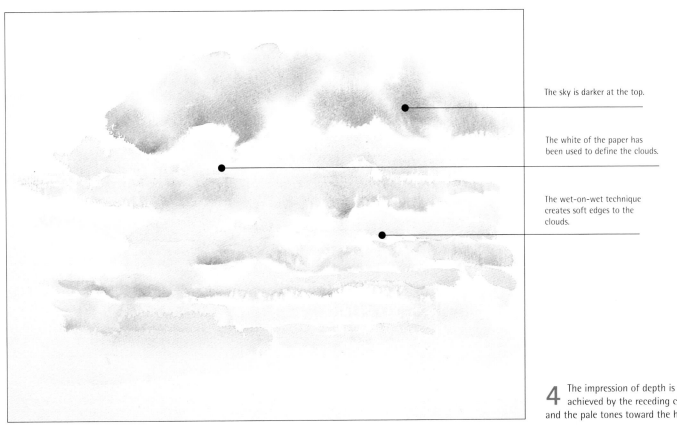

The sky is darker at the top.

The white of the paper has been used to define the clouds.

The wet-on-wet technique creates soft edges to the clouds.

4 The impression of depth is achieved by the receding clouds and the pale tones toward the horizon.

Q76 How do I paint clouds?

A | **Clouds are integral to any landscape, seascape or skyscape painting.** They are important compositional devices, used to balance the picture or to suggest depth and recession. In order to paint them convincingly, you need to be able to recognize the three general shapes and be familiar with the best methods of rendering them. Take care not to look directly at the sun.

Clouds fall into three main categories: cirrus are high clouds with wispy, feathered edges that often appear in bands converging at the horizon; stratus clouds are lower layers of soft grey cloud often accompanying rain; cumulus clouds are soft and fluffy, with a triangular shape that is whiter on top with a shadowed underside.

Clouds are rarely pure white. Being three-dimensional, clouds may show light from the sun on top, rendered by using a small amount of raw sienna, or even Naples yellow. Underneath they will be a more neutral cool colour, showing their volume and any shadows.

There are several ways of rendering white clouds against a blue sky. Lifting off (see Question 39) is one option, but with confidence, retaining white areas of the paper will show watercolour off at its best. One method is to dampen the sky area with a sponge, occasionally leaving random dry areas where the clouds are formed. Apply a generous amount of colour wash, using a large brush, such as a mop brush, and try to be direct and do not use too many brushstrokes. Clouds are only vapour and rarely have hard edges, so the next washes are critical and are best done quickly before the water dries. The type of paper should also be considered. A smooth, hot-pressed paper will give good 'runs' but washes may dry with hard edges.

Cirrus, or mare's tails, can be achieved by laying a flat wash in cobalt blue, for example, and when dry apply a very 'wispy' gouache white mix, applied with a dry brush or even with a feather.

A backlit cloud with the sun behind, appears to have a halo of light. I painted these clouds using ultramarine, yellow ochre and a mix of delft blue and ultramarine violet with a touch of burnt umber, using a smooth hot-pressed paper that gave a defined edge to the wash when dry.

For the soft, fluffy cumulus clouds of a summer's day, paint around the cloud shape then add light washes on the underside to give a sense of depth and dimension.

Q77 How do I paint sunsets?

A The setting sun is always an attraction for the painter, but there can be a danger or temptation to produce a predictable 'sweet' image. Painting any sky will entail working quickly, as every minute there will be changes in colour or cloud formations. A photograph, of course, will capture a moment but recording, observing and rendering a picture in watercolour will, in time, improve your confidence and visual memory.

Your choice of colours will vary from sunset to sunset – observe closely as not all sunsets are red and orange, but more likely to show tints of pinks, greys and mauves occasionally moving into warmer pinks and oranges. Make use of backlit clouds to give the impression of glowing light and render the landscape as a near silhouette to give the impression of approaching evening.

Transitional techniques such as wet-on-wet and blending are ideal for achieving subtle changes of colour and tone. Lay gradated or variegated washes to begin with and wash the colour into them.

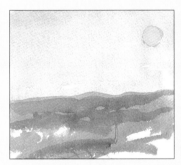

This early evening landscape is bathed in the mauve tones of approaching dusk. The setting sun has a warm, pink glow, achieved by lifting off the sky wash and then applying a light pink wash of alizarin crimson to the circle of white paper.

I used very subtle changes of colour on a smooth paper, to show the glow of a fading sunset along the horizon. By blending raw sienna with touches of alizarin crimson, wet-on-wet, the bands of colour merge behind the silhouetted clouds.

Q78 How do I paint stormy skies?

A As with any sky study, speed is of the essence when trying to capture the drama of a storm. Storms can manifest themselves in various ways, from towering thunder clouds, known as cumulonimbus, which contain a mass of water and usually produce heavy rain or hail, to stratus clouds. A really dark storm cloud behind an urban landscape can be very dramatic.

A stormy sky is the most exciting subject to paint in watercolour, giving the opportunity to apply wet washes, sometimes tilting the paper to produce 'runs' and back-runs, some accidental marks with hard edges, some soft. Effects can be enhanced by the choice of paper – a hot-pressed paper is my preferred surface for cloud and storm effects.

I lifted off streaks of wash from these dark rain clouds, to give the impression of drifts of rain. The neutral grey of the clouds is broken along the horizon with bands of brighter highlights, suggesting the sun breaking through the clouds.

I used a smooth, hot-pressed paper for this quick study of an approaching storm. I dropped a darker, wet wash onto the underlying layer, leaving the paint to blend and dry with a hard edge, defining the shape of the cloud.

Q79 How do I paint seascapes?

A | **Seascapes have provided inspiration to many artists through the centuries.** On a fine day the sea and beach can be the most pleasant place to paint. Subjects are limitless – the texture of rocks, pebbles, the detritus of seaweed, driftwood and fishing nets are all a great attraction. Don't overlook harbours or seaside resorts. Ships and boats of all shapes and sizes are wonderful subjects and the colour of a lively seafront makes an interesting study.

The sea itself is an ever-changing phenomenon, with rolling or crashing waves, surf and foam, and a constantly shifting surface that can sparkle with dancing light in sunshine or reflect the flat, dull colour of a cloudy day. When painting the sea, break your composition down into simple areas: sky, horizon, waves, surf, calm water and beach. See Question 81 for painting white water and foam. A spattering or stippling technique is ideal for the texture of sand and pebbles along the water's edge. To achieve a sense of recession in a calm sea, paint the waves at closer intervals as they recede toward the horizon.

Wet-on-wet and blending techniques (see Questions 33 and 34) suit the shifting motion of the sea.

Shells are beautiful subjects for close-up studies. Either combine wet washes with pencil line drawings or use a smooth paper working wet-on-dry, for crisper details.

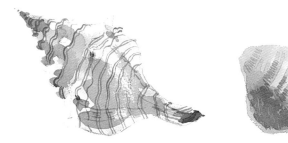

The beach is a wonderful place to set yourself up to observe and paint. Here, the wooden beach huts, palm trees and figures made for an interesting subject, full of the intense light of the bright sunshine in Key West.

In this picture, painted in Cromarty, Scotland, my eye was caught by this windswept scene, with the lighthouse in the background and the boat adding interest.

This seascape uses a variety of techniques, from wet-on-wet for the sky and cliffs, to spattering and resist techniques for the details of the pebbles and spray.

I used masking fluid for the white foam and spattered paint across the foreground for the pebbles on the beach.

The rolling motion of the breaking waves is reinforced by following the shape of the wave with the brushstrokes and using darker washes underneath the waves.

Q80 How do I paint moving water?

A| Studying the way water moves and reacts to light is a fascinating pasttime in itself and painting moving water is one of the more challenging and difficult exercises in watercolour. You will need to note the direction in which the water is moving, the shape and extent of any ripples, the effect of light and reflections, and decide what techniques to use to represent falling or splashing water.

The moving concentric circles made in a fountain trough are a good place to start when studying water. You will encounter reflections and splashes of water in an easily contained and attractive subject. Spattering masking fluid will create random 'splashes' of water, and a thin line of masking fluid drawn with a reed pen can be used to represent a trickle or flow of water. You can transfer these techniques to larger scale subjects, such as waterfalls, leaving the white of the paper to represent the cascading white water, painting in lines of neutral tones of grey and blue to give depth to the water falling behind the spray.

Ripples are a subtle indicator of moving water. They will move in concentric circles where water flows into a pool, or will break the surface of a calm lake or river where a breeze moves across the water. White highlights mark the top of ripples and can be used to give the impression of dappled light.

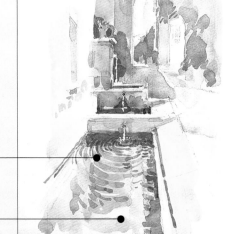

A darker tone was used beneath the water line and in the shadow areas.

The ripples of water reflect colours from the building and sky.

6 Continue to work on the reflections and shadows in the water troughs, using the darker mix from Step 5 to follow the shadowed area under the water level. Finalize the darker tones on the foliage, the darker the mix the greater the contrast with the lighter areas. Rub off the masking fluid to reveal the water flowing between the troughs.

Project

MATERIALS   Rough paper 140lb (300gsm), 5B pencil, masking fluid, reed pen, large squirrel brush, No. 8 round brush, watercolour paints

The gently cascading water between these stepped water troughs makes for a pleasing composition, incorporating moving water, ripple effects and reflections.

1 Plot the main elements of the composition with a 5B pencil, marking the concentric circles of the water ripples in the lower trough. Using a reed pen dipped in masking fluid, 'draw' the lines of the running water between the troughs.

2 Mix a light wash of Naples yellow and apply as an undercolour with a large squirrel brush. Drop a little light red into the wet wash to give a warm ochre colour to the building on the left, and a very light wash of cobalt blue for the sky. Use some of the colour to introduce the reflection of the sky in the water trough. Allow to dry.

3 Mix a clean ochre colour from raw sienna and apply to the buildings and along the shadow side of the trough, to show the reflection of the buildings. Mix sap green and burnt umber for the waterline and stone markings behind the taps.

4 Next, mix a warm shadow colour from alizarin and ultramarine violet, and apply to the building and the cast shadow on the ground. For the ivy covered building on the right, mix sap green and burnt umber, applying a darker wash wet-on-wet for the leaves and plant pot.

5 Using the green mix from Step 4, add a little raw sienna and apply to the water troughs, following the water line and the edge of the shadowed area in the top trough. Add touches of the colour over the reflected blue sky on the right of the lower trough and follow the concentric circles of the water ripples.

Q81 How do I paint rough water?

A **Rough, or white, water is found in crashing waves, waterfalls and rapids.** There are several techniques that you can employ to suggest the bubbling foam. For seascapes, mask out any white water or foam at the top of a wave, or where the breakers hit the beach, using a spattering or stippling technique with masking fluid. Build up the darker tones of the waves and look for the darkest blue-green tones in the shadow areas in the smooth water beneath the waves. You can also use free brush marks or the dry-brush technique for the broken waves, or add opaque white to heighten the effect.

In waterfalls or rapids, look carefully for repetitive shapes in the fast-flowing water, you may discover quite linear patterns where the water falls or gushes between rocks. Use a resist technique to maintain the white of the paper and follow the shape of the flowing water with neutral colours to give it depth. You can also lift-off streaks of colour from a wet wash, or blot off rounded shapes for a wider area of spray.

I captured the drama of this breaker crashing into the sea wall using a few simple washes and painting around the white paper to represent the spray.

I painted the sky first, leaving the white paper to represent the breaking wave.

Q82 How do I make water appear transparent?

A | **The transparent nature of watercolour paint makes it ideally suited to water studies.** But to give the impression of looking into water you need to carefully observe the different elements before proceeding. For example, looking into a rock pool you will see reflections, light on the surface and the shapes of the objects below the surface. Any ripples across the surface will make the objects beneath appear distorted and larger. Refraction causes shapes to change beneath the water surface and you will need to note this carefully.

The transparent nature of water can be conveyed with a simple wash over the top of the objects below. Keep colours clean with just one or two glazes. To give the impression of light reflecting off the surface, use sgraffito or masking fluid to suggest sparkles and highlights.

The reflection of the boat is rendered in a strong green to suggest the form of the boat beneath the surface.

White or light highlights have been left between the 'waves' to give the impression of sunlight on water.

Q83 How do I paint reflections in water?

A The nature of reflections depends on the water surface – from a mirror image on still water to distorted shapes on a rippled surface. The colour of the reflected image should be darker and muted, and its shape softer. Look for other colours too, such as those of the sky and passing clouds.

A reflected image in still water will be seen directly beneath the object, following the same proportions. Objects further away from the water's edge will not be reflected to their full height.

An image reflected in rippled water will be fragmented and its shape will become faceted. The effects of broken colour (see Question 44) can be used to make horizontal brush marks simulating movement in water reflections. The wet-on-dry technique is suited to painting reflections, giving you control over the shape of the image.

To practise a mirror image simulating still water, place a toy boat on a small mirror and observe the angles of reflection.

The water in a harbour is often calm and the reflections are likely to be relatively clear. I painted this boat using muted tones for the reflection. Remember that any lettering will be reversed in a reflection.

The reflection of this building has been distorted by the ripples on the water surface and only a subtle suggestion of the white facade is discernible. The colours of the reflected trees and bushes along the shoreline are slightly muted tones, with soft, blurred edges rendered wet-on-dry over the ripples of the water surface.

Q84 How do I paint buildings?

A | A barn, farmstead or distant village are elements that appear in landscapes and become important factors in your composition. Townscapes clearly involve the inclusion of buildings and you may wish to make a particular building the central theme of your painting. The enormous variety of architectural styles is a fascinating subject for the artist itself and you may find that you fill much of your sketchbook with studies of window details, stonework, carvings and doorways.

To render the three-dimensional aspect of a building accurately, you will need to have a basic understanding of two- and three-point perspective (see Question 61). Choose your viewpoint carefully and ensure that all the lines lead in the correct direction towards the vanishing point. To help to judge the proportions of the building accurately, use a measure to check off the position of windows and doors: hold a pencil at arm's length and measure off the depth of a window, for example, with your thumb. Hold this measure against other features, such as doors or the roof, to judge the proportions.

The solid outlines of buildings require some definition which is best achieved by working wet-on-dry. A smooth paper will give you a clean line, too. Brush-ruling (see Question 51) can be used for roof lines and eaves, or patterned brick or stonework. Look for shadows cast under eaves and in windows to give a sense of depth to a flat surface. Buildings are often textured, with plasterwork and brickwork: use wet-on-wet effects and blending to add texture, or use a rough paper combined with dry brushstrokes. For fine details of window panes and reflected light, use masking fluid or tape to retain the white of the paper, applying a light, neutral wash over the white once the painting has dried.

A windmill is a charming building in any landscape but its cylindrical shape is quite a challenge. Use darker tones to suggest the curve of the wall as it moves away from you.

I 'drew' around the window frames using a small, fine brush.

The fine detail of the windows and doors of the station facade in Lagos, Portugal, called for a detailed pencil drawing and then applying light areas of colour with the point of a fine brush.

Different dilutions of the same wash are used for the glass roof.

The fine detail of the ironwork is rendered in pencil.

This quick sketch of the old railway station at Strathpeffer was made in pencil on a smooth paper. The simple colour washes highlight the main features.

HIGHLAND
MUSEUM OF
CHILDHOOD

Q85 How do I paint interiors?

A As a subject, an interior study is perhaps one of the more practical and convenient for the artist – a glimpse through a doorway, the corner of the studio or living room – and is ideal when the elements and seasons force you indoors. Your subject matter is virtually endless and you will hone your skills in painting patterns, textiles, wood, glass and stone.

A basic knowledge of perspective (see Question 61) is important when painting interiors, together with an understanding of how to light your subject – whether to use natural light from a window (which will change throughout the day) or artificial light. Select your composition carefully, as you would with a landscape or still life study, and try different formats and crops.

The warm colours of the rug lead the eye into the picture, toward the light of the window beyond.

The doorway is used to frame the view beyond.

A view through a doorway to a room with a window beyond, makes a good exercise in tonal values.

Q86 How do I paint flowers?

A | **Flowers are a firm favourite with all artists.** There are many ways of painting flowers, from highly defined and detailed botanical studies to the 'freer' approach using techniques with broad brushes and wet-on-wet marks for looser interpretations. However, generally you will want to convey the shapes and colours of a bouquet and this involves searching out nature's 'geometry'.

Make pencil studies of different flower heads, petals and leaves. You will notice that circles, cones and ovals are common and they can be used as a generalized shape on to which you can add detail. Lightly draw a circle or arc to follow the extent of the petals and paint within this line to follow the natural symmetry of the open flower.

Many watercolour techniques are suited to flower studies but you will need to add some different colours to your palette (see Question 17), in order to capture their vibrancy. For still lifes, use a darker background tone behind the flowers to help throw them forward and enhance the flower shape.

I chose to use a smooth paper with wet washes for this study of an iris stem. The resulting loose shapes, with clear edges, perfectly matches the delicate nature of the petals.

Using a slightly darker wash of Winsor violet, I dropped the colour on, moving the wet paint to follow the shape of the petal.

The smooth, inexpensive paper results in crisp outlines that define the shape of the stem.

Sunflowers are delightful subjects. The flower heads are very symmetrical, with wonderful bursts of colour in the petals and strong, graphic leaves. I used a dark background to highlight their shape, painting wet-on-dry to retain the crisp outlines.

Q87 How do I paint still lifes?

A | A still life painting requires skills in composition, pattern and texture, lighting and colour balance.
In composing a format for a still life, the juxtaposition of objects will be a factor in making a 'calm' or 'tense' picture. Objects touching the edge will give tension, a classical triangular composition can create calm. Remember that the unfilled spaces are as important as the drawn areas.

A group of objects can be set up easily: bottles, vases, books, kitchen utensils, fruit, vegetables and flowers are often close to hand. Keep the arrangement simple and check the main elements in a thumbnail sketch. Diagonals, verticals and horizontals will help to give rhythm to the group. Light the set up with a light source from one direction and note how the shadows affect the composition. Consider your background carefully – a plain, neutral background will help to focus on the still life. You could use a toned paper to establish a similar midtone before you start to paint.

A fresh fish is simply rendered in pencil and wash. The bright highlight provided by the lemon draws the eye into the image, keeping it clean and simple.

A close-up study of the potting shed makes for an interesting still life.

Project

MATERIALS Handmade rough paper 250lb (410gsm), HB pencil, No. 2 squirrel brush, No. 6 round brush, watercolour paints

When setting up your composition, choose your background carefully in order for the main elements to be seen clearly and to avoid any distracting and unwanted detail. I selected a plain, neutral-coloured board that toned with the warm hues of the bowl and tablecloth.

1 Lightly sketch in the main elements of the composition with an HB pencil. Look carefully at the shape of the fruit and draw an ellipse for the circular bowl seen in perspective. Note the general shapes of the folds in the tablecloth. Then add initial washes of colour; mix cadmium orange for the grapefruit, gamboge and cadmium orange for the bowl and apply with a No. 2 squirrel brush. Drop some cadmium red wet-on-wet for the shadows on the grapefruit.

2 Use a light wash of cadmium yellow for the lemon, following its shape with the brush and leaving white paper for the highlights. Apply a light wash of burnt umber for the shadows falling across the cloth. This helps to establish the form of the folds. Darken this wash with a little ultramarine violet for the blue tone in the shadows.

3 Add initial colour to the peach with a mix of alizarin and cadmium red. Use a touch of ultramarine violet dropped wet-on-wet for the bloom on the top side. Mix a rich purple for the plums from alizarin, delft blue and a little ultramarine violet. Darken this mix further with more delft blue. Drop cobalt blue wet-on-wet for the bloom on the plum's skin.

4 In order to keep the whole painting moving at a similar pace, start to work on the background colour using a mix of raw umber and burnt umber, warmed with a touch of light red. This immediately helps to give depth and throw the fruit bowl forward. Return to the fruit, adding the blackcurrants in the foreground with a mix of delft blue, Payne's grey and ultramarine violet, the redcurrants with cadmium red and the apricots and nectarine in the bowl with a light wash of cadmium orange.

5 Add detail to the pattern on the tablecloth, following the checks and stripes where they are distorted and broken by the creases and folds. Use a shorthand for the overall pattern rather than attempting to include every detail.

The bloom on the plums was added by dropping paint wet-on-wet.

The checked pattern of the tablecloth helps to accentuate the creases and folds.

6 Continue to strengthen the washes on the fruit with stronger mixes of colour using a higher proportion of pigment to water. For the lemon, mix cadmium yellow and raw umber, using a darker mix on the shadowed side and adding a little stippling to give texture to the surface. Add a few finishing touches to pull the painting together. Apply a mix of ultramarine violet and cobalt blue for the shadow under the table, to help anchor the picture.

Q88 How do I paint metal objects?

A | The colour and shine of metal surfaces present some unusual challenges for the artist. Both the amount of shine on the surface and the strength and direction of the light source will affect the myriad reflections that give form. Metal will often reflect colours and textures of adjacent objects too – blend these colours into the overall patterns on the metal surface.

The contrast and sharpness of light and shade will establish how shiny the objects are. Metal reflects very bright spots or highlights, that can be described by leaving the white of the paper. Use a wet-on-dry technique to define these areas, using a brush with a good point. Alternatively, mask off the highlights at the start of your painting using a resist technique (see Question 53). Before setting up a still life with metal objects, try different lighting positions to vary the strength and dominance of the reflections.

Some metal objects have dull, worn surfaces. For the subtle changes of colour on burnished copper or a rusty iron, use wet-on-wet and blending techniques. Establish the colour temperature of the metal. Chrome, silver and aluminium have a cold, blue, neutral tone whereas brass and gold have warmer tones. Copper contains many colours, both warm and cool.

Your subject matter can be derived from a wide selection of household objects.

This sketch of a motorcycle includes different textures of chrome, rubber and leather. I 'drew' the finer details with a No. 8 sable brush with a good point, leaving the 'whites' to simulate the shine of the metal.

Q89 How do I paint glass objects?

A | Glass presents similar challenges to metal objects for the artist, with the exception of its transparency. This should be considered an advantage for the watercolourist, enabling you to use layers of transparent washes to build the subtle changes of tone. Glass is available in many different forms, from clear to coloured, handmade to cut crystal. When painting glass objects you will need to take a very careful look at your subject, noting the highlights, any reflections and any colours both reflected in the glass and cast in the shadows. Clear and coloured glass objects should be approached differently.

Clear glass objects are defined by the colours and objects surrounding them. Start by painting the background first and any adjacent objects, or those behind the glass. A dark background will enhance the clear glass objects. Use masking fluid or leave highlights of white paper to define where the light hits the edge of the glass. You can suggest form by subtle blending of tones within the shape of the glass. Look for ellipses in round objects.

When lit from behind or from the side, coloured glass will appear illuminated with a transparency that is ideally suited to watercolour. Build layers of colour with light washes, remembering to carry the colour into the shadows in a slightly muted tone.

For still lifes with glass objects, try to keep the set up simple – a few different shaped glasses, one filled with water, will created distorted shapes. Consider the lighting. Try different positions with an artificial light and if using natural light from a window, bear in mind that reflections will change dramatically if the sun should go in, and that shadows will change as the sun moves.

In this simple still life, I used the background colour to define the shape of the objects, leaving the white of the paper to represent the edges and rims of the wine glasses.

Q90 How do I paint clothes and drapery?

A Approach textiles and clothes as you would any subject that includes areas of light and dark tone, using the shadows to convey form. Look for the gravitational pull of the fabric, often accentuated by strong vertical lines along folds. Creases give subtler indications of what lies underneath and will either be pulled taut or gently swag.

Every type of material will fall and crease in its own way, for example wool falls in soft, undulating folds, whereas cotton and silk will accentuate the underlying form in a more positive way, with the points of stretch and stress accentuated with sharper lines. A coat thrown on a chair will fall in a different way to one worn by a model. In each case, look for the pulls of the fabric to define the underlying object. Folds often form repetitive shapes, such as a 'V' or 'W', use the shadows or negative spaces to define their shape.

On a clothed figure, look for where the fabric pulls across the joints, for example folds are more concentrated in the crease of an elbow or behind the knee. Skirts often fall in swathes of material, with strong vertical folds in a standing figure, or with concave creases if the model is seated. Before attempting a clothed figure, practise painting simple drapery folds with a piece of material draped on a chair or hung from a hook.

Patterned fabric clearly presents its own challenges. Use a shorthand for a complicated pattern, using random marks. Patterns can help in assessing the direction of folds and creases – stripes or checks are good patterns to practise with.

I used a smooth paper for this sunlit portrait, which gives smoother lines and finer details. The shape and pattern of the model's dress is only loosely suggested, with darker, denser washes in the shadow areas.

The shape of the skirt is suggested by a darker wash following the shadows.

The checked pattern of this cloth helps to establish the shape and direction of the folds.

Q91 How do I choose a pose?

A | **Many professional models will assume poses naturally – either standing, sitting or lying.** You can refine this further by choosing a head and shoulders or three-quarter length view, a back view or side profile. When selecting a pose, always consider how comfortable it will be for your sitter to maintain for any length of time and how easy it is to resume after a rest.

Different poses lend themselves to different formats and compositions. A long, reclining figure suits a landscape format, a standing figure is naturally vertical and a seated figure is often triangular in composition. This pose is perhaps the most common and has endless variations. Always make quick thumbnail sketches of your composition before you start to paint.

This full-length, seated pose is comfortable and relaxed.

This seated figure follows a classic 'L' shape composition. I painted the pose direct, with no underdrawing, as the model couldn't hold the pose comfortably for any length of time.

These two poses show alternative approaches to the same subject. It is worth trying different poses until you find one that both you and the model are happy with.

The extended legs gives this pose an unusual landscape format.

Q92 How do I paint figure studies?

A | **Figure drawing is a whole subject itself and needs a lot of practise, but there are many benefits for the watercolourist.** A basic understanding of the proportions of the figure and how to convey balance will help you to add convincing figures to your paintings, and a more detailed look at facial features and anatomy will enable you to paint figure studies and portraits with confidence. Watercolour is one of the more unforgiving mediums for these subjects, as corrections and alterations are difficult to achieve.

Start by assessing the proportions of the figure. Use the head as a guide – an average adult can be divided by the head height 7 to 7.5 times. The proportions of babies and young children will differ (see Question 93). Next, assess where the centre of balance lies – look for the position of the head, shoulders and pelvis. A line drawn from the centre of the head to the ground will help you find the centre of balance. When the weight is shifted onto one leg, the shoulders will tilt up and the pelvis will tilt down in a counter direction to compensate.

A figure drawing class will help you to gain confidence but by simply observing, drawing and painting, you will soon master the human figure. Fill a sketchbook with figures in different situations – at the bus stop, sports events, a café or at home.

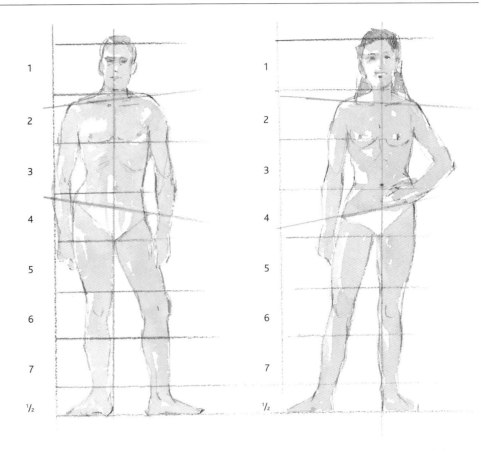

The proportions of an adult can be assessed by dividing the figure by the head height.

These poses illustrate how to convey balance by establishing the centre of balance and the compensating tilt of the shoulders and hips.

I quickly sketched these figures at work in a fish market, using light pencil marks to outline the main shapes and overlaying simple washes to build form.

Q93 How do I paint children?

A | **Children make delightful subjects – but they don't stay still for long!** You will need a good deal of patience and to be well-prepared before you start. The key to accurate painting of figures is proportion, and children follow slightly different rules until their late teens when they reach adult proportions (see Question 91). Using the head as a measure, a baby has a relatively large head in proportion to its body, approximately a quarter of its body length. As they grow older, the head size does not increase relatively, but the torso and legs grow.

You may be tempted to use photographs to paint from, but I would only recommend this as reference material and never as a substitute for pencil and brush. Make quick sketches and try painting from life to capture the moment and character of the child.

To make your child's portrait convincing, you will need to judge the proportions accurately. The body of a baby or toddler is approximately 4 times the head height, a young child approximately 5½ times. A young teenager is approaching the adult ratio of 7 times head height.

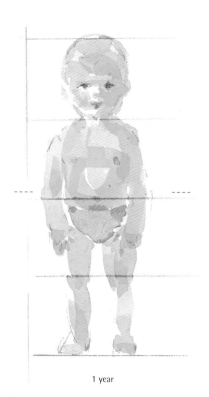

1 year

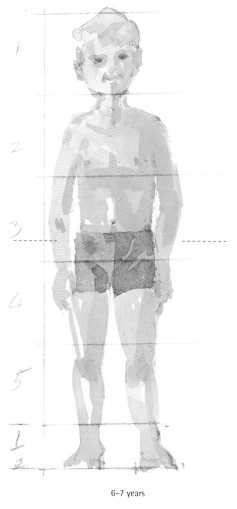

6–7 years

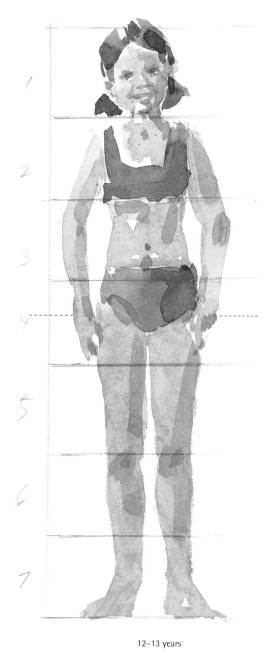

12–13 years

-------- middle line (halfway)

This head study of an older child uses simple washes of alizarin crimson and raw sienna, with touches of cadmium red, to render the fresh complexion.

Very young children have rounded heads and bodies, all circles and curves.

Informal poses, such as when children are playing or absorbed in a task, are much easier to paint than a formal pose – but you will have to work quickly!

Q94 How do I paint portraits?

A | For an accurate portrait, you need to have a basic knowledge of anatomy and the proportions of the head. Think of the head as egg-shaped, with a vertical axis for the centre of the face and horizontal axes for the eyes and mouth. These structural lines become elliptical when the head is turned.

The proportions of the head are divided into three segments: the hairline to the eyebrow; the eyebrow to the tip of the nose; the tip of the nose to the bottom of the chin. Another useful measure is to place the eyes halfway and the mouth halfway between the tip of the nose and the chin. The corner of the eye is level with the top of the ear. These proportions will vary with age and ethnic group but are useful guidelines.

Lighting is an important factor to consider, together with the pose (see Question 91). A backlit portrait, or *contre-jour*, will add drama to the picture. A portrait need not be simply head and shoulders, of course – full-length, seated or three-quarter views are all options.

A portrait is not just about correct facial features, you need to aim to capture something of your sitter's character, too. You can do this with props that relate to personal interests, clothing and the setting. Talk to your sitter as you paint and you will be rewarded with a relaxed and animated expression.

For this relaxed portrait I combined pencil and wash, using a fine brush to draw the striking facial features once the initial wash had dried.

Loose, wet washes follow the shape of the body.

For this portrait of an Arab Berber, I used a pencil underdrawing, adding watercolour to emphasize his features and the unusual clothes.

Project

MATERIALS Smooth hot-pressed paper 140lb (300gsm), 5B pencil, No. 8 squirrel brush, rigger brush, watercolour paints

A smooth, hot-pressed paper will give you crisper outlines for
the more detailed painting that portraits require.

1 Lightly sketch the outline of the figure with
a 5B pencil, starting with the head and hair
and then the shoulders. Find the centre of the
face and add the position of the eyes, then
nostrils and mouth. Lightly shade the tonal
areas, such as beneath the eyes and under
the cheekbones, to establish the light source
and give form to the face.

2 Mix a thin wash of light red and raw sienna
for a warm skin tone and apply to the whole
figure, leaving a few highlights. Apply a darker,
denser wash beneath the chin, nose and cheeks
and continue this colour down the arms. Add a
touch of alizarin to the face for a warmer tone
to build form.

3 Apply an underwash of burnt umber and
light red to the hair, using loose, wavy lines
to follow the pattern of the curls. The shape
of the hair helps to outline and give form to
the face.

4 Use a light wash of terre verte on the face,
adding burnt sienna to build a darker skin
tone. Build up another tonal layer on the hair
using a mix of ultramarine, raw umber and burnt
umber. Add details to the eyes to indicate their
position and the direction of the model's gaze.

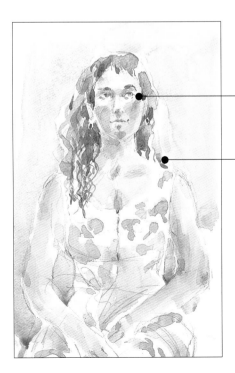

The gaze of the model's eyes
suggests a point of interest
beyond the picture frame.

The soft curls of hair help to
frame the face.

5 Continue to work over the entire figure,
building shadows under the chin and along
the cleavage. Add shadows on the light-coloured
dress with a wash of terre verte, following the
natural indentations and shape of the body
to give substance to the figure. Add the pattern
on the dress with suggestions of colour. Finalize
the curls of hair using a rigger brush. Finally,
apply a light wash of raw sienna to the background
around the figure to place it in context.

Q95 How do I paint a self-portrait?

A | **There are different ways to approach this subject.** You can try to paint your reflection in a mirror or use a photograph as reference material. When looking in a mirror your image will be reversed and you will not see yourself as others see you. In order to achieve an exact likeness, you need to set up two mirrors at right angles, so that the first reflection is reversed in the second mirror. This method will take some practise and experimentation, as any slight movement of the head will change your viewpoint. You could try drawing a grid on the mirror and another on your paper to help plot your portrait. Draw the main features in pencil or sanguine Conté pencil first and then use the underdrawing to add watercolour at a more relaxed pace.

Think about the lighting and setting. A strong, front light will show you in a harsh and honest light but a soft, side light is more flattering. As with any portrait, think about your pose and whether to include any props in the setting.

I painted this self-portrait by looking at my reflection in a mirror positioned directly in front of me. I've included the background setting of my studio and used a three-quarter view, rather than a head and shoulders pose.

The light source is directly behind me, creating a rim of light around my figure.

I used a sanguine Conté pencil for the initial underdrawing.

Q96 How do I paint pale flesh tones?

A | Mixing colour for flesh tones needs a good eye for observation and a broad palette that includes not only warm colours, but a selection of cooler hues, too. Pale skin tones vary enormously and you will only occasionally need a pale pink. Flesh colour varies across the body, it is warmer at the body's extremes, such as the ears, hands, knees and feet, and cooler in fleshier areas such as the stomach. Skin will reflect colours from its surroundings, appearing warm in a warm artificial light and cool in daylight. Clothes and any immediate surroundings will also cast shadows and reflected colours onto the skin.

Start with a pale, neutral wash. Painting wet-on-wet to blend colour needs courage but when dry, you can build layers of secondary and tertiary washes with drier washes to describe the shape and form of the body. Use a broad brush, such as a No. 8 or No. 10 round, to follow the sweeps and curves of the figure.

Suggested colours for pale flesh tones include: light red, raw sienna (or yellow ochre), burnt sienna and alizarin crimson. Terre verte – a very muted, thinly pigmented earth green – is a good colour for underpainting and for shadows. A limited palette will prevent colour mixes from becoming muddy.

I used terre verte for the cooler highlights towards the base of the back, with warmer tones of light red and a touch of alizarin crimson to follow the form.

Q97 How do I paint dark flesh tones?

A | Dark skins don't show as many obvious differences in colour temperature across the surface of the body as pale skins (see opposite), but changes may still be detected if you are keenly observant.

A suggested palette for dark skin tones may include: burnt umber, sepia and alizarin crimson, together with ultramarine violet for deep shadows.

For this portrait study I used burnt umber, sepia and alizarin crimson.

The face is given depth and form by layering glazes of colour to build tone.

Q98 How do I paint domestic animals?

A | Pets are extremely popular subjects and a good place to start before moving on to more unusual species. Although animals can be a specialized discipline, they can be a very rewarding subject for the watercolour painter and will help you to practise your skills of observation to record movement and the texture of fur and skin.

A good exercise to start with is to use a medium brush and to paint direct, obscuring the anatomical details and simply following the overall shape. Pets may not stay still for long, so be prepared to cover a large sheet of paper or your sketchbook with a series of studies of different poses. Some will be more finished than others, and some will be disappointing, but the practise will be worth it. Look for overall shapes of the body and head, cats are often very rounded whereas dogs appear more angular, sometimes with triangular heads and muzzles. For more detailed study of different animals, visit wild life centres and look at animal anatomy.

The different textures of skin and fur are a wonderful opportunity to use different watercolour techniques. Wet-on-wet and blending lend themselves to soft fur, use masking fluid to retain white patterns or patches, lifting off can be used to soften edges, and fine details of long fur or whiskers can be added with a rigger brush.

I painted the markings on these cats wet-on-dry to give some definition to the pattern. I was particularly attracted to the triangular composition created by the pose.

I used a pencil to outline the basic pose, making quick sketches and then adding the colour washes later.

This study of a sleeping cat uses passages of blended colour to capture the subtle changes across the fur.

Q99 How do I paint horses?

A Equestrian painting is a very specialist subject beyond the scope of this book and will require detailed study if you wish to pursue the topic further. However, horses make interesting subjects for the general watercolourist and you may come across them in your travels or wish to include them in a landscape painting.

The key to most figure studies, be it animal or human, is proportion and horses in particular need to be correctly proportioned to reflect balance. Take a measure holding a pencil at arm's length – the head for example – and see how many times it fits into the height and breadth of the horse. Look for overall shapes; face on, the head is coffin shaped, with two inverted triangles joined at the base with their apexes removed, and the body is cylindrical with rounded haunches.

Use quick, direct painting with limited brushstrokes to capture the immediacy of a moving horse, observing the gait and position of the feet. A visit to an equestrian event or a race meeting will provide a great source of inspiration.

The white of the paper has been left to represent the pattern along the horse's nose.

Working horses are majestic and you can often observe and paint them at country shows. I used a few simple brushstrokes to give solidity to a pencil underdrawing, leaving white highlights for the gleam of their coats and the ruffles of hair around the hooves.

Q100 How do I paint birds?

A| Birds are another extensive subject that requires further study if you wish to paint them in detail. However, with a little background knowledge of anatomy, observation of movement and a few painting techniques for texture, you will be able to develop your skills.

Start with studies of stuffed birds in natural history museums, looking at the anatomy, head shapes, wing shapes and feet. Then, observe live birds at zoos or bird sanctuaries, or in your garden or the park, making quick studies and noting colours and shapes. Ducks, chicken and geese make delightful subjects – ducks are a simple oval shape and chickens are triangles. Feathers can be gathered quite easily and are very decorative, making interesting studies in their own right.

A variety of techniques can be used to paint birds: wet-on-wet for soft impressions of feather masses, wet-on-dry for clearer details of wings and plumes, and clean lines with a rigger brush for wing patterns.

The intricate and pronounced feather configuration on these crested screamers drew my eye.

I used dry brushstrokes to follow the shape and pattern of the chicken's feathers.

I chose these flamingos for their elegant shapes and unusual colours.

Project

MATERIALS Arches hot-pressed paper 300lb (640gsm), HB pencil, No. 6 round brush, fine rigger brush, watercolour paints

I gathered this mix of feathers at a children's zoo. The different sizes, shapes and colours make for an interesting study. A smooth paper will allow to you draw finer details and sharp edges.

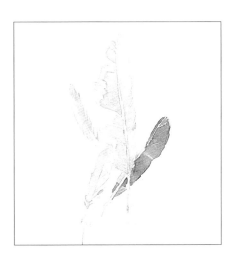

1 Lightly sketch the outline of each feather with an HB pencil, indicating the spines and where the feathers separate.

2 Mix a wash of burnt umber and Payne's grey and apply this with a No. 6 round brush to the large goose feather. Follow the shape with sweeps of the brush. Darken the mix slightly with ultramarine violet for the shadow on the right. Work on the feather on the right, darkening the wash with Payne's grey. For a soft gradation of tone, lift off some of the wash with a tissue or apply a lighter wash, working wet-on-wet.

3 Next, work on the flamingo feathers on the left. Mix a light wash of cadmium red and cadmium orange and apply to the top feather, leaving a white line down the middle for the spine. Blot off some of the wash at the base. Use a very thin wash of the same colour for the lower feather to suggest a blush of pink. For the soft fluff at the base, use a light wash of Payne's grey.

4 Start to add finer details. Use burnt umber for the spine of the large feather, 'drawing' the line with the fine point of the brush. Use a pale wash of yellow ochre for the quill at the base. Add the fine individual feathers, following the sweep with your brush. Use a shorthand for groups of strands rather than drawing each one. **Inset:** Continue to work in the same way on the pigeon feather on the right.

5 Move back to the flamingo feathers and add a darker wash of cadmium red. Add the shadows with a wash of Payne's grey and ultramarine violet.

6 Use a rigger brush to paint the fine details, again following the shape of the feather. Look for subtle changes in colour, using washes with more pigment to strengthen the hue.

Q101 How do I paint fish?

A **Fish are wonderful subjects for still lifes, with their sparkling scales and variety of colours.** You will need to work quickly and if you haven't finished in one painting session, wrap them well in ice and store in the refrigerator to keep them looking (and smelling!) fresh. Look at the variety of fish at your fishmongers: mackerel have striped markings, red mullet have defined scales and shell fish, such as crab and lobster, have wonderful mottled markings and vibrant colours which make interesting studies on their own.

Moving fish are more of a challenge, seen through the transparent and refracted layer of water they are often just quick dashes of colour. An aquarium is a good opportunity to paint some more colourful varieties and will help to improve your visual memory.

Wet-on-wet techniques lend themselves to the subtle blending of colours over the skin. In order to capture the sheen of fish scales, use thin transparent washes, leaving white highlights. Detailed pattern of scales can be added with a fine rigger brush wet-on-dry. A smooth paper will give crisper outlines.

I used simple strokes of colour to follow the shape of the head, leaving the white of the paper for the eye and adding the black eyeball later.

I dabbed on dashes of colour over an initial wash for the pattern of the trout's scales.

Fishermen are very patient. If you have a friend who fishes, go with them to paint – their equipment, their poses, casting or just sitting – make interesting studies in their own right, and, of course, you can record the catch of the day.

Glossary

Aerial perspective – an artistic principle that conveys a sense of depth in landscapes by exploiting the natural atmospheric conditions where objects appear cooler and less distinct toward the horizon.

Alla prima – a method of painting directly onto the paper without the use of an underdrawing, using simple washes and completing the painting in a short time frame.

Blending – a method of merging different colours or tones on the paper so that the transition between the two is subtle.

Body colour – an opaque watersoluble paint that can either be mixed with watercolour or used on its own to create opaque colour, adding highlights or painting light over dark.

Broken colour – a painting technique where pure colours are placed next to each other to create a third colour in the viewer's eye.

Complementary colours – the colours that lie opposite each other on the colour wheel. They enhance the vibrancy of each colour when placed next to each other in a painting.

Distressing – a method of disturbing the surface of the paper to create texture or to lift off colour. See also sgraffito.

Dry-brush – a technique that drags a dry brush with little paint across the paper surface to give texture and uneven colour.

Glazing – the application of layers of washes or brushstrokes to build tone and define form, each layer is applied once the underlying layer is dry.

Gouache – see body colour.

Linear perspective – an artistic principle that creates the illusion of three-dimensions on the flat surface of the paper by exploiting the fact that objects appear smaller in the distance and that parallel lines converge at a point on the horizon.

Masking – the application of a resist medium, such as tape or fluid, that protects the surface of the paper from overlaid washes.

Monochrome – a painting technique that uses tones of a single colour to complete the image.

Negative space – the space between the solid, positive shapes of the subject.

Overdrawing – a technique where pen or pencil lines are drawn over the watercolour wash.

Palette – the surface on which washes of colours are mixed. Also, the choice of paint colours used in a picture.

Pigment – the ingredient of paint that imparts colour, it can either be derived from natural products or manufactured synthetically. Some pigments adhere to the paper surface more strongly than others.

Primary colours – red, yellow and blue. These colours cannot be mixed from other colours.

Resist – a medium that is applied to the paper surface to protect it from overlaying washes. Masking fluid and masking tape are resists that can be removed once the paint has dried, to reveal the white of the paper beneath. Candle wax and oil pastels applied to the paper surface will resist watercolour washes for a more textured effect.

Secondary colours – orange, green and violet. These colours are mixed from pairs of primary colours.

Sgraffito – a distressing technique that adds texture to the paint surface by scraping with a sharp scalpel or blade.

Spattering – a method of adding texture by flicking paint across the paper surface.

Sponging – a painting technique that uses a sponge to apply paint colour to the paper surface, creating a textured or mottled effect.

Stippling – a method of applying dabs of paint using the round tip of a brush to create a pattern of dots.

Tertiary colours – (1) a range of colours created by mixing a primary with its adjacent secondary colour, for example blue with green to give a blue-green, or turquoise, or red with violet to give a warm purple. (2) Tertiary is also a term used to describe colours that are created when two secondaries, or a primary and its complementary colour, are mixed to create muted, neutral hues.

Thumbnail sketch – a quick, small sketch to assess different compositions and formats.

Tone – the relative lightness or darkness of a colour.

Underdrawing – a method of drawing the main elements of the composition before applying paint, either to use as a guide for different washes or as an integral part of the painting adding definition to detailed areas.

Underpainting – a method of outlining the main forms of the subject using paint, often in a single colour, that will complement the subsequent colour washes.

Vanishing point – the point in linear perspective where parallel lines converge on the horizon.

Wash – a thin layer of diluted watercolour paint applied to the paper with a brush or sponge. A flat wash is applied evenly; a gradated wash changes from light to dark; a variegated wash combines washes of different colours.

Wet-on-dry – a painting technique in which a wash or brushstroke of colour is applied on a dry surface or over a dry wash and dries with a defined edge.

Wet-into-wet – a painting technique in which paint is applied into a wet wash or onto wet paper. The paint will move on the paper surface to give soft, blurred edges and blend to give transitional colours.

Index

acid-free paper 13, 70
acrylic paint 64
aerial perspective 79, 124
alla prima 49, 55, 114, 124
animals
    horses 119
    pets 118
architecture
    brush-ruling 66
    techniques 102–3
artist's quality paints 20
atmospheric perspective 79
autumnal scenes 90

babies, painting 112–13
back lighting 80
back run 57
balance, figure studies 111
beaches 96
birds, painting 120–1
black, use of 37
blending
    medium 62
    technique 51, 124
'blooms' 57
blotting paper 24
body colour 21, 124
    see also gouache
broken colour
    for painting water 101
    stippling 60
    technique 59
brown wrapping paper 16
brush-ruling technique 66, 102
brushes
    basic equipment 12
    caring for 5
    choosing 17
    uses of 18–19
buildings
    interiors 104
    painting techniques 66, 102–3
burnt sienna, granulation effects 62

candle wax, resist techniques 68
caring for equipment 25
cats, painting 118
'cauliflowers' 57
children, painting 112–13
Chinese brush 18–19
Chinese white 21, 70
clothes, painting 109

clouds
    lifting out technique 56, 94
    painting 92–3, 94
    stormy skies 95
cold-pressed paper 13, 14
colour wheel 28–9
coloured paper 16
colours
    black 37
    flesh tones 117
    greens 34–5
    limited palette 30, 55
    luminosity 70
    mixing 28–9, 34–5, 36
    monochrome 39
    neutrals 36
    selecting 7, 32
    shades, tints and tones 38
    'temperature' of 33
    see also paints
complementary colours 28, 70, 124
composition
    figure studies 110
    of painting 74–5
    still lifes 106
concentrated watercolours 20, 70
contre-jour lighting 80, 114
cool colours 33
correcting mistakes 57, 71
Cotman, John Sell 6
cotton buds 24

dark flesh tones 117
distressing 58, 124
dogs, painting 118
domestic animals, painting 118
drapery, painting 109
drawing, underdrawing 48
drawing board 12, 24
dry-brush technique 54, 124
drying time, speeding up 45
Dürer, Albrecht 6

easel 12, 24
egg tempera 70
equestrian painting 119
equipment
    additional 24
    caring for 25
    getting started 12
    outdoor painting 24–5

eraser 12
evening light 83

fabric, painting 109
fan brush 18–19
feathers, painting 121
figure studies
    animals 118–19
    children 112–13
    colours 32
    flesh tones 117
    opaque effects 21, 70–1
    portraits 114–15
    poses 110
    self-portrait 116
    techniques 111
fish, painting 122–3
flat brush 18–19
flat wash 40
flesh tones
    dark 117
    pale 117
flower paintings
    colours 32
    techniques 105
focal point 74
foliage, painting 88–9, 90
foreshortening 78
formats, composition 74
French ultramarine, granulation effects 62

Girtin, Thomas 6
glass objects, painting 108
glazing technique 53, 124
glycerine, for texture 62
gouache
    figure studies 71
    opaque effects 7, 21, 64, 70
    snow scenes 91
gradated wash 41
granulation effects 62
greens, mixing 34–5
gridding up 77
gum arabic 71
    for texture 62

hairdryer, for drying paint 45
horizon line 78
horses, painting 119
hot-pressed paper 13, 14
hue 38

interiors, of buildings 104
iridescent medium 70

kitchen paper 24
kraft paper 16

landscape format 74
    figure studies 110
landscapes
    aerial perspective 79
    colours 32
    mountains 87
    painting 86
layering washes 44
leaves
    autumnal scenes 90
    painting 88–9
lifting out
    snow scenes 91
    technique 56
lighting
    bright sunlight 84
    effects 80–1
    evening 83
    portraits 114
    time of day 82
limited palette 30, 55
linear perspective 78, 124
luminosity 70

masking fluid
    for painting water 98
    resist techniques 24, 68–9
    for spattering 61
masking tape 24, 68–9
masking technique 124
media, types of 64
metal objects, painting 108
mirrors, self-portrait 116
mist, conveying 90
mistakes
    correcting 71
    washing off 57
mixing colours 28–9
monochrome 39, 81, 124
mop brush 17
mountains, painting 87
moving water 98

negative shapes 77, 124
neutral colours 36

oil pastel, resist techniques 64, 68
opaque effect 70–1
opaque white 21
outdoor painting, equipment 24–5
overdrawing 64, 65, 124

paints
    choice of 8
    concentrated watercolours 20
    pans and tubes 20
    running 45
    see also colours
pale flesh tones 117
palette, for mixing colours 12, 124
palette of colours 8
    limited 5, 30
    selecting 32
pans of paint 20
paper
    choice of 7, 13, 24
    coloured 16
    size of 76
    stretching 15
    toning 43
    weights of 14
patterns, of fabric 109
Payne, William 81
pencils
    basic equipment 12, 24
    overdrawing 65
    watercolour pencils 22–3
perspective
    aerial 79
    buildings 102
    interiors 104
    linear 78
    mountains 87
pets, painting 118
pigment 124
plaka 64, 70
pointillism 60
portrait format 74
portraits
    flesh tones 117
    painting techniques 114–15
    poses 110
    self-portrait 116
poses, figure studies 110
primary colours 28–9, 124
projects
    feathers 121
    flat wash 40

gradated wash 41
layering washes 44
lifting out 56
light and shade 81
limited palette 31
moving water 98
opaque effect 71
portraits 115
resist techniques 69
shadows 85
skies 93
still lifes 107
stretching paper 15
trees 89
underpainting 49
variegated wash 42
wet into wet 50
proportions
    adults 111
    children 112
    of head 114
putty eraser 12

rain, conveying 90
reed pen 98
reflections
    metal objects 108
    self-portrait 116
    in water 101
resist techniques 7, 64, 68–9, 124
    seascapes 96–7
    snowscapes 91
rigger brush 18–19
rough paper 13, 14
round brush 17, 18
ruler, brush-ruling technique 66, 102
running paint 45

salt crystals, textured wash 62–3
sandpaper
    for distressing 58
    for snow scenes 91
scale of painting 76
seascapes, painting 96–7, 99
secondary colours 28–9, 124
self-portraits 116
Seurat, Georges 59
sgraffito 58, 124
shades, of colour 38
shadows
    evening 83
    and light 80–1

painting 85
shells, painting 96
side lighting 80
Signac, Paul 59
size of painting 76
sketchbook 13, 24
skies
    clouds 94
    painting 92–3
    stormy 95
    sunsets 95
sloping easel 12
snow and ice, conveying 91
spattering
    seascapes 96–7
    snow scenes 91
    technique 61, 124
sponge
    equipment 24
    for lifting off 56
    use of 60, 124
square format 74
squaring up 77
squirrel brush 17
still lifes 106–7
stippling 60, 124
stool, for outdoor use 24
stormy skies, painting 95
stretching paper 15
sunlight
    bright 84
    dappled 81
sunsets, painting 95

techniques
    basic 26–45
    painting 46–71
'temperature' of colours 33
tertiary colours 28–9, 124
textiles, painting 109
texture medium 62
textured wash 62–3
thumbnail sketches 74, 124
time of day
    evening 83
    lighting 82
    sunsets 95
time of year
    autumn 90
    winter 91
tints 38
tips 20, 45, 78

tones 38, 124
toning, paper 43
toothbrush, for spattering 24, 61
top lighting 80
townscapes 102–3
transparency
    of glass 108
    of water 100
trees
    autumnal scenes 90
    painting 88–9
tripod easel 12
tubes of paint 20
Turner, JMW 6, 21
Turner's blue paper 16

underdrawing 48, 124
underpainting 49, 124

vanishing point 78, 124
variegated wash 42
viewfinder grids 77

warm colours 33
washes 6–7, 124
    adding texture 62–3
    flat 40
    glazing 53
    gradated 41
    layering 44
    variegated 42
    wet-on-wet 50
    white areas 67
washing off 57
water
    moving 98
    reflections 101
    rough 99
    seascapes 96–7, 99
    transparent 100
water pot 12
watercolour pencils 22–3, 64
waterfalls 98, 99
waves, painting 99
wax, resist techniques 68
weather
    clouds 94
    rain and mist 90
    skies 92
    stormy skies 95
weights of paper 14
wet-on-dry

for reflections 101
    technique 52, 124
wet-on-wet
    alla prima 55
    painting mountains 87
    seascapes 96–7
    technique 50, 124
white
    clouds 94
    leaving areas of 67
    paint 21
    snow scenes 91
Winsor and Newton, Artist's Quality pans 8

Acknowledgements

Author's Acknowledgements

I would like to thank Katie Hardwicke for her help in collating and editing, and Roger Bristow for his idea in conceiving this book, together with the companion *Drawing Solutions*.

I would also like to thank the Symington family in Oporto for their kind hospitality, which inspired the Portuguese images in this book.

Publisher's Acknowledgments

The publisher would like to thank Ben Wray for the photography, Tom Green and the team at Grade Design Consultants, George Taylor for additional photography, Gemma Wilson and Margaret Binns.